D1558724

The Primal Vision

JOHN V. TAYLOR

The Primal Vision

❯❯❯◆❮❮❮

Christian Presence Amid
African Religion

Introduction by
M. A. C. WARREN

FORTRESS PRESS
PHILADELPHIA

Library of Congress Catalog Card Number 64-11228

General Introduction

>>>◇<<<

CHRISTIANS are being presented by the contemporary world with what is, in many ways, a unique opportunity of demonstrating the Gospel. Scarcely less unique is the opportunity being offered to them of discovering in a new and deeper way what that Gospel is. Those are large claims. Can they be justified?

What is this unique opportunity? At the very least it is the opportunity presented to Christians to demonstrate the fundamental truth of the Gospel that it is a universal message, whose relevance is not limited to any one culture, to any one system of thought, to any one pattern of activity. That is by no means the truism that it may appear to be. For more than four centuries the expansion of the Christian Church has coincided with the economic, political and cultural expansion of Western Europe. Viewed from the standpoint of the peoples of Asia, and to a growing extent from that of the peoples of Africa, this expansion has been an aggressive attack on their own way of life. Quite inevitably the Christian Faith has for many in these lands been inextricably bound up with this Western aggression. But it has also to be admitted quite frankly that during these centuries the missionaries of the Christian Church have commonly assumed that

Western civilization and Christianity were two aspects of the same gift which they were commissioned to offer to the rest of mankind.

This assumption was sometimes quite conscious and was explicitly stated. More often it was quite unconscious and would have been indignantly denied. But in neither case are we called upon to judge our fathers. Their sincerity can hardly be disputed. Their self-sacrificing devotion finds its monument today in the world-wide diffusion of the Christian Faith, the existence, in almost every country of the world, of a community of Christians recognizably part of the Universal Church.

What we are called upon to recognize is that in the world of our time there is a widespread revolt against any form of domination by the West. Nations whose political independence was only achieved 'yesterday' or is only about to be achieved 'tomorrow' can be excused for having their own interpretation of the past, an interpretation unlikely to coincide with that which is prevalent in the West. This very waning of Western influence is in part our Christian opportunity. We are freer today than we have ever been to serve the Gospel without the risk of confusion between that Gospel and the 'power' of the West.

But that is not all. The peoples of Asia and Africa, in their revolt against domination by the West, are presenting a specific challenge to the Christian Faith. In what does this consist?

There are three main ingredients in this challenge.

First there is a critical evaluation of the Christian

6

religion which rejects it as something inherently Western, as something which fails to correspond to the *felt* needs of Asia and Africa. Christianity is, in such judgement, altogether too Western in its character and in the form which it assumes in its local manifestations. This rejection is the more serious in that Asian and African peoples are themselves, like us in the West, confronted by the bewildering demands of the modern world. All the old landmarks are disappearing. Everywhere there is a desperate search for some inner basis of security, some inner assurance which can enable men and women to face the storm. In the sequel, particularly in Asia, but not only there, the peoples of these countries are seeking to find this psychic security by digging deep into their own past. This is at once an expression of their revolt against the West and one explanation of the renaissance of the great ethnic religions. Further to this it is to be noted that in a new way these ancient religions are becoming themselves missionary. No longer content to be on the defensive, they are offering themselves as answers to the questionings of mankind.

Here is a situation which is new. Only once before, and then in its earliest centuries, has the Christian Church had to face a comparable challenge to its claim to meet the deepest needs of man's heart and mind. The devotees of Mithras, the mystery cults of the Mediterranean world, the Gnostics in that earlier day were serious competitors with the message of the Gospel. Their appeal failed. There followed the long thousand years during which Europe was isolated from the rest of mankind and built

7

for itself its own peculiar civilization. Then suddenly, drawing on its inner dynamism, a dynamism closely related to its faith, the European world overflowed its narrow boundaries and began its great expansion. For a time it appeared as if nothing could arrest this expansion. It is of some importance to recognize that it is by no means certain that anything can! The scientific view of the world, with all its implications about human survival, is Western in origin. Communism and nationalism are Western concepts. It may well be doubted if anything can arrest the advance of all mankind towards something like a common civilization – if common destruction is avoided. Nevertheless there is, at the moment, a significant pause in the impetus of Western expansion in its Christian expression. The challenge to Christians is precisely this that the ethnic religions as well as secularist philosophies of life are offering themselves as the basis of the new world civilization. Both deny the relevance of Christianity.

The *second* challenge follows from the first. Can the Christian Faith not only prove its ability to meet the deep human needs of our time but also make peoples of different cultural backgrounds feel at home in the new world? This is a more complex task than would appear. For it is part of our paradoxical situation that, at a moment when the world is becoming so obviously interdependent, every nation in it is seeking to assert its own independence. And religion and culture are the means by which independence is asserted. Has the Christian Church got a Gospel to meet this situation? We may put the question this way – can the Christians of the West accept the fact that the expression which Christianity will receive in its Asian and African forms may well be, almost certainly will be, in many respects very different indeed from what we know in the West? That again could be worded as follows – are we of the West prepared to trust the Holy Spirit to lead the Christians of Asia and Africa, or must a controlling Western hand be permanently resting on the Ark of God? Let no one imagine that those questions will find an easy or unanimous response from Western Christians.

There remains a *third* challenge. The Christian Church has not yet seriously faced the theological problem of 'co-existence' with other religions. The very term seems to imply the acceptance of some limitation of the universal relevance of the Gospel. Can that be accepted? It can hardly be doubted that the answer must be 'no'. Are we then shut up to the alternatives of what in some disguise or other must be an aggressive attack on the deeply held convictions of those who live by other Faiths than our own?

This book, originally one in the *Christian Presence Series*, has been designed to express a deliberate recognition of the challenge outlined above and to suggest that there is a way in which they can be met without any betrayal of the Gospel – indeed in deeper loyalty to that Gospel's real content.

First of the demands presented to us by this understanding of the contemporary world is a *glad* acceptance of the new situation in which the Christian Faith can

9

everywhere be distinguished from its past historical association with Western political, economic and cultural aggression. Here is the 'great new fact of our time', every whit as great a fact as the existence of the Church in every land. Here is our great new opportunity, even though it may well be an opportunity to witness through suffering. The Cross, after all, was not a symbol of imperial domination but of the *imperium* of sacrifice. The Christian Faith has nothing to lose by suffering. In and through suffering it can perhaps speak home to the hearts and minds of suffering mankind better than in any other way.

Second of the demands upon us, to march with our gladness, is a deep humility, by which we remember that God has not left himself without witness in any nation at any time. When we approach the man of another faith than our own it will be in a spirit of expectancy to find how God has been speaking to him and what new understandings of the grace and love of God we may ourselves discover in this encounter.

Our first task in approaching another people, another culture, another religion, is to take off our shoes, for the place we are approaching is holy. Else we may find ourselves treading on men's dreams. More serious still, we may forget that God was here before our arrival. We have, then, to ask what is the authentic religious content in the experience of the Muslim, the Hindu, the Buddhist, or whoever he may be. We may, if we have asked humbly and respectfully, still reach the conclusion that our brothers have started from a false premise and reached a faulty conclusion. But we must not arrive at our judgement from outside their religious situation. We have to try to sit where they sit, to enter sympathetically into the pains and griefs and joys of their history and see how those pains and griefs and joys have determined the premises of their argument. We have, in a word, to be 'present' with them.

The present volume essays the ambitious task of offering some clues to what is happening in that spiritual conflict which is modern Africa. For spiritual conflict it is and that in its essence. The very cry of '*uhuru*', 'freedom', is only in a derived sense a word of political or economic significance. It is by accident, tragic no less for being an accident, that it has racial overtones. The cry is wrung from the heart of what Laurens van der Post has described as 'a battle about being and non-being; about having a soul of one's own or not having a soul at all'. The cry may not even be directed against foreign dominion because it may just as well spring straight from the heart of an African who is the citizen of a politically independent country. It is important for us to understand this or we shall fail to understand that Africa of tomorrow, when all Africa may have achieved political freedom, but in which Africans will still be seeking 'uhuru'.

The spiritual conflict in Africa is a striving to re-establish that primal unity of man with both the material and the spiritual universe which African man instinctively feels to be true 'being', and which hardly exists anywhere in Africa today. Believing this, the author

11

seeks to establish first of all the essentially African way of
feeling the truth about things, a 'feeling after the truth',
which finds expression in an illimitable anthology of
proverbial sayings rather than in any systematic philosophy. To get at this feeling one has to be present with
the African, living with him and entering into his world
of thought. This Mr Taylor has done in a way not given
to many and it is out of his own intimate knowledge of
Africa and of rich friendships with many Africans in
different parts of the continent that this book is written.

Africa is a vast continent and all generalizations about
Africa and Africans must be suspect. But we can find
tracks into the forest, the enchanted forest of Africa, a
world which the West only enters in its dreams. This
book charts some of these tracks. One African translation
of John 1.16 in a literal rendering into English would
read, 'We have all received grace following hard upon
grace': and the picture is of a procession of people thread-
ing their way single file along a bush or forest track.
Certainly along the tracks marked here there is evidence
that the grace of our Lord Jesus Christ is to be found at
the heart of Africa's primal vision.

> *Lift the stone and you will find me*
> *Cleave the wood and I am there.*

That is not pantheism but the claim of the Omnipresent,
full of grace and truth, in the fellowship of whose service
is 'uhuru'.

M. A. C. WARREN

12

Contents

1

Classroom Religion

Omuggo oguli ewuwo tegugoba ngo (Ganda)
*When the leopard comes to you, the club at your neighbour's
won't drive him off*

>>>◊<<<

THAT devastating Ganda proverb should, perhaps, be
enough to check any more non-Africans from offering to
interpret Africa to the world. Fortunately a growing
number of Africans are taking on the task and I can aim
to be at best a bagman retailing their products. Even that
I would not attempt to be were it not for a sense of
urgency in the search for the true meeting-place where
Christ is conversing with the soul of Africa. And I take
courage from the conviction that one necessary qualifi-
cation for the stranger who wishes to speak is to know
how little he has understood. That, at least, I have learned
in many bitter lessons.

Some years ago I lived for several months in a thatched
hut close to a rather remote bush school in Uganda. I had
finished breakfast one morning and was ironing some
clothes when the children came out of the schoolroom at
the end of their morning prayers. I watched them spread
out over the field, aimlessly ambling or chasing each
other as though it were the end rather than the beginning
of the day's work. True, seven little boys and a girl were

15

setting off purposefully along a track that wound into the elephant grass as though they were under orders of some kind, while in front of the classrooms one part of the shifting throng seemed to be resolving itself into two files under the casual direction of an older boy; but they behaved as though they had all the time in an endless summer day in which to do the next thing on the time-table. The staff presumably were in conclave for they had not yet emerged from the schoolroom.

A girl in a gentian blue frock broke away from the rest and came across the path towards my hut. I bent over the shirt on the table and a moment later there was a shy tap on the open door. During the exchange of salutations at the threshold she remained half hidden behind the doorpost, but when I had invited her to come in, she slipped past me and in one flowing, silent movement was seated on the mat in the corner of the little room, her legs tucked sideways out of sight under the blue dress. As I gave her the formal indoor greeting, cool finger-tips brushed mine and for one instant she looked up and around with the devouring curiosity of a child. Then the eyes were downcast, the slender hands lay still in her lap, and she leaned one shoulder against the lime-washed wall, as relaxed as a young antelope asleep in the sun.

She looked about twelve years old. I was often to see her racing with other children on the school field, climb-ing with long strides to the stony top of the ridge, sweat-ing with her hoe under the early morning sun; yet she never lost that extraordinary quality of stillness which so

16

many African women seem to possess. Incongruously I thought of Keats.

> *Thou still unravished bride of quietness,*
> *Thou foster child of silence and slow time . . .*

I went on with my ironing.

It was one of those models which work with paraffin and a pressure pump. It makes a continuous small hiss, a comfortable purring sound, and after a few minutes I noticed that my visitor's eyes were following my hand to and fro with puzzled fascination. Then she caught sight of the little blue flame of burning vapour inside the shoe of the iron, leant forward to make certain she had seen aright, and a longdrawn *Haa* of wonderment escaped her lips. She glanced up, saw that I was watching her, and embarrassment wrestled with curiosity across her face. 'Do you see the fire?' I asked.

'Yes. It is a marvel.'

'It burns with paraffin like a small primus stove.'

Her face lit up and she laughed for the joy of comprehension. Then she relaxed again into her former position, no longer shy but quiescent and companionable. It is an unfailing wonder and delight, this tranquillity of human relationships in Africa. Whether it be child or adult makes no difference; one can enjoy the other's presence without fuss or pressure, in conversation or in silence as the mood dictates. Whether the task in hand may be continued or must be left depends upon a score of fine distinctions which the stranger must slowly learn; but one thing is certain – a visitor is never an interruption.

'Thank you for working', she murmured.

'I'm working. But now I am near to finish.'

'That is good.'

I asked her what class she was in. She told me Primary 2. It seemed very low for a girl of her age but I knew there could be many reasons for that. 'Where do you live?' I asked her then.

She looked surprised. 'Don't you know me?' She laughed again, richly enjoying the moment, for now she had the advantage of me. Then quickly she was demure again and gentle. 'I live at Wambogwe.'

I had been there several times but no chord of memory stirred. 'I am ashamed. I don't remember your face. What is your name?'

'Nantume.'

Still no light. I cursed myself for a boor and a fool as I had done so often and was so often to do again. She stood up and moved towards the door.

'I have seen you, Sir. I must go back to school.' And with that she was gone.

An hour later the headmaster was drinking coffee with me and making good the deficiencies of my memory. It appeared that we had called to see Nantume's father on our way to the landowner's house the previous Saturday. Her father was out but we had sat and talked for ten minutes with his wife, a bedraggled, morose woman, and Nantume had come forward to greet us. I vaguely remembered a girl in a shapeless grey digging-frock who had squatted under the eaves watching us, but my main recollection was of extreme squalor. Later we had come upon the father at a beer drink, supporting another wretched creature who was vomiting at the side of the path. Nantume had called on me this morning to repay my visit to her parent's home.

Her own mother had grown tired of the drunken father many years before and had run away to live with a man of a different tribe. Nantume and her younger sister would not see their mother again. Since then two other wives had joined the homestead. One was a daughter of the landowner, but from my knowledge of his household I was not surprised to hear that she was illiterate and without religion, nursing only enough pride of family to make her husband and his daughters wretched with her scorn. The second wife, of another tribe, was the one I had met at their house, and she was childless.

I glanced out of the window towards the school where I could see the children at their desks through the open classroom doors. In the evening they would go home. The neat coloured frocks, the smart white shirts and khaki shorts, would come off, not thrown untidily on the bedroom floor as an English child's might be, but folded away in a small wooden suitcase. And the children would emerge again from the huts dressed in the drab, tattered garments of home. Down they would go to the valley with pitchers and paraffin tins to draw the household water; or off to the banana grove behind the house to dig till sunset; or up to the cool winds of the ridge to bring the goats or cattle in from grazing. And if I met them there, these shabby unkempt children, I might not know them, being acquainted only with their groomed and schoolroom selves.

This might well be the most terrible failure of the whole Church in Africa – that it meets people only in their best clothes. Those who can see the children only in their uniforms, the clergy only in their robes, the ordinary people only in some 'Christian' context, are unlikely to plan or preach or legislate with much wisdom or relevancy. Such Christianity becomes something to be put on at certain times and in particular circumstances, and has nothing to do with other areas of life.

For forty years and more the advance of the Christian Church in tropical Africa has depended more upon her virtual monopoly of Western education than upon any other factor. Today secular governments are taking that monopoly from her and it is a bitter irony that the factor which seemed to be Christianity's greatest strength in Africa threatens to prove its heaviest liability. For to a great extent it has become a classroom religion. In many tribes the word used to signify Christian worship means simply 'to read', and believers are the same as literates. The Gospel has been presented by instruction but there has been little appeal to sympathy and imagination; the sermons have vastly outnumbered the symbols, even in the Roman and other Churches of a 'Catholic' emphasis. Christianity has come as a daylight religion of reason and reasonableness set over against the darkness of super- stition. By defining the conflict in those terms it has won its inevitable victories and at the same time ensured that they should be only partial, not the total victory of him

20

who is Lord of the dark as well as of the day. By confining the Kingdom of God within the protective walls of the conscious and the rational it has left untouched the great deep of the subliminal, and unredeemed the glories of the elemental energies of man. The incalculable has been left out of account, the supernatural played down, the mystery glossed over. This too-cerebral religion has no answer for young Africa when she cries

> . . . *My God, my God, but why should I tear out my*
> *Shrieking pagan senses?*
> *I cannot sing your anthem nor dance it without swing,*
> *Sometimes a cloud, a butterfly, or a few drops of rain are*
> *on the window of my boredom.*
> *She drives me incessantly through the space of time.*
> *My black blood pursues me into the solitary heart of night.*[1]

This is the inner significance of the complaint that Christianity is the white man's religion. It is bad enough that religious pictures, films and film-strips should have almost universally shown a white Christ, child of a white mother, master of white disciples; that he should be worshipped almost exclusively with European music set to translations of European hymns, sung by clergy and people wearing European dress in buildings of an archaic European style; that the form of worship should bear almost no relation to traditional African ritual nor the content of the prayers to contemporary African life[2]; that

[1] Leopold Sedar Senghor, *Chants pour Näett*, translation by Sango-dare Akanji.

[2] It is ludicrous, for example, that peasant congregations of the Anglican Church in parts of Africa should still pray by name for

21

the organizational structure of the Church[1] and its
method of reaching decisions[2] should be modelled ever
more closely on Western concepts rather than deviating
from them. But in the last resort these are all merely
outward forms that could quite easily give place to others.
They are serious because they are symptoms. They persist
because they are the school uniform of a classroom religion reflecting a world-view that is fundamentally
European.

But the tides of reaction are running strongly and the
prospects for a white man's religion in the Africa of
tomorrow are negligible. Even the most loyal of the
African leaders of the Church are deeply aware of that
fact. Dr Busia, for example, one of the outstanding
Christian laymen of Africa, deeply concerned for the
progress of the Gospel, finds that he has to describe the
Churches as 'alien institutions' in Ghana,[3] while Fr
Meinrad Hegba, a Roman Catholic priest in Dahomey,
says:

Some shrewd observers notice with anxiety, among many

members of the British Royal Family but not for their own chiefs or
political leaders.

[1] See F. B. Welbourn, *East African Rebels*, pp. 203, 211.

[2] A significant example of the contrast in method emerged
during the preliminary planning of the first All Africa Churches'
Conference, held at Ibadan in 1958. British and American 'experts'
had agreed that this was to be Africa's conference run in Africa's
way. But when it appeared that the African leaders intended to have
no agenda but to allow the findings to emerge from free, informal
discussion, the experts felt constrained to take a hand, and once
again Western methods prevailed!

[3] Christian Council of the Gold Coast Report, *Christianity and
African Culture*, Accra 1955, p. 54.

Classroom Religion

Africans, an embarrassment, a mistrust, unconscious or overt, towards Christianity. The period of delirious enthusiasm which welcomed the first preachers of the Gospel is over. Now, in proportion as faith grows in depth and breadth, a corrosive discontent ventures to call everything in question. The masses are faithful to Christ and the Gospel, praise God. But will they always resist the climate of uneasiness which is being created and maintained by the exciting new awareness, both individual and collective, of the African personality?[1]

Attending to the outward forms of Christianity is not unimportant. Indigenous music is at last beginning to win respect as a vehicle for Christian worship; murals, sculptures and tapestries by African artists have adorned some of the church buildings; drama and dancing have made a tentative appearance in the liturgy and in the communication of the Gospel in a few places. African leadership is making its influence felt in the mission-founded Churches and many are looking at the independent Churches no longer to condemn but to learn from their emphases.

Yet in all this a warning light flickers from the fact that the enthusiasts are mainly non-Africans. This can only partly be explained by the conservatism of African clergy. The real reason is that the white 'indigenizers' are too superficial, and Africans know it. How many of the missionaries and teachers who have fun with African hymns and paintings recognize that a truly African worship is going to seem queer and distasteful to European Christians? How many have any conception of the pro-

[1] Meinrad Hegba, 'Christianisme et Négritude', essay in *Des Prêtres Noirs s'interrogent*, p. 189.

23

fundity of the difference between the Western and the African world-view, or, if they realized it, could accept the validity of the African? The hesitancy of many Africans to share our enthusiasm for indigenization stems from their unspoken question: Do they know what they are asking for?

Christ has been presented as the answer to the questions a white man would ask, the solution to the needs that Western man would feel, the Saviour of the world of the European world-view, the object of the adoration and prayer of historic Christendom. But if Christ were to appear as the answer to the questions that Africans are asking, what would he look like? If he came into the world of African cosmology to redeem Man as Africans understand him, would he be recognizable to the rest of the Church Universal? And if Africa offered him the praises and petitions of her total, uninhibited humanity, would they be acceptable?

> *From the despair of our cry,*
> *The heart's intensity,*
> *Out of death and dereliction*
> *In the land of our uprootedness,*
> *We shall one day give birth to our Christ,*
> *A Christ made flesh of our flesh,*
> *Our dark flesh of the black people.*
>
> *On that day when we are wholly yours,*
> *Our Lady of the Black World,*
> *All the rhythm of our songs,*
> *All the rhythm of our bodies –*
> *O Lady of the Black World –*
> *Yes, all the rhythm of our dances,*

Classroom Religion

> *Exulting in the Spirit*
> *And in Our Lady who is altogether black,*
> *Will be as the rhythm of eternity.*[1]

Is that expectation of another African priest merely sentimental, or may there be a profounder meeting than has hitherto been recognized, a more face to face and mutual encounter between Christ and the 'pagan' soul? What would happen if the Christian presence were set more humbly and attentively in the midst of the *Présence Africaine*? That is the question that this book attempts to answer.

[1] Gerard Bissainthe, 'Prière de l'Homme Noir à Notre-Dame du Monde Noir', poem in idem, p. 282.

2

Through Other Men's Eyes

Atanayüta atenda nyina okufumba (Ganda)
He who never visits thinks his mother is the only cook

>>>◇<<<

THE following chapters will deal almost exclusively with different aspects of African traditional religion and of that way of looking at things which persists as an inarticulate philosophy in many individual Africans long after the old religion itself has been discarded. The title of this book uses the more general term 'primal' in recognition of the fact that so many features of African religion occur elsewhere in the globe and in the history of human belief that we may reasonably claim that we are dealing with the universal, basic elements of man's understanding of God and of the world.

The word 'primitive', except, oddly enough, when applied to the Church, has taken on too much the sense of backwardness to be applicable in this context. It is too suggestive of the popular but largely invalid transference of evolutionary theory to the realm of human ideas, and subtly rules out any thought that one may discern the self-revealing Logos and Light of God in the insights, experiences and values of this interpretation of the world. The profounder conversation that we have envisaged between the Christian and the pagan mind will be im-

26

possible so long as the former talks down as if to a child.

But is it possible to speak of African Religion as if it were one and the same throughout the continent south of the Sahara? Certainly there is not one homogenous system of belief throughout Africa. One tribe gives prominence to an element which is only vaguely conceived in another. In several ways the traditional culture of the whole Niger basin reveals a sophistication and an individuation that is not known elsewhere. Nevertheless anyone who has read a number of ethnological works dealing with different parts of Africa must be struck not only by the remarkable number of features that are common but by the emergence of a basic world-view which fundamentally is everywhere the same. To quote an Akan proverb, Man's one speech has thirty varieties but they are slight.

It may further be objected that, even though there has been such a thing as African Religion, it is so much a thing of the past, so disrupted and discredited by its encounter with the modern world, that to approach it as if it were one of the 'higher' religions is to indulge in a fiction. Dr Michael Gelfand, for example, one of the most sympathetic students of African traditional ritual, writes:

For the proper conduct of the Shona religion the person practising it must live in close contact with his rural environment where beer can be brewed and, when necessary, an animal sacrificed. . . . Is it possible to come to any conclusion regarding the chances of survival of this tribal religion? If it is to be judged by the fate of Druidism, Huna or the ancient Greek

27

and Roman religions, I believe that its prospects are small and that, for each year that passes by, less and less of the ritual is being carried out. . . . The most significant fact is that the educated man is hardly ever seen at one of the Mashona religious ceremonies.[1]

Few would deny that the influence of the old beliefs is much less than it was. But before it is dismissed as a spent force there are three aspects of the question that should be remembered.

First, probably about seventy per cent of the 135 millions in Africa south of the Sahara are neither Muslim nor Christian. That alone should be reason enough for taking their traditional religion seriously.

Second, that traditional world-view is continually reflected in the thoughts and attitudes of Christian Africans. Dr Gelfand with great insight says of the African of Mashonaland, 'He can believe in his own religion without necessarily practising it, and at the same time be a practising Christian.'[2] That is undoubtedly true of thousands of good Christians in all parts of Africa. But in addition to them there is the mixed multitude described by Dr B. A. Pauw when he comments that

a simple and clear-cut grouping, into Christians or church people on the one hand and pagans on the other, is not possible because of the existence of a considerable but undefined middle 'group' consisting of people who claim to be church adherents but have no official church connections.[3]

Both in that spiritual no man's land between the two

[1] M. Gelfand, *Shona Ritual*, p. 12.   [2] Idem, p. 2.
[3] B. A. Pauw, *Religion in a Tswana Chiefdom*, p. 8.

28

religions and in the thinking of perhaps the majority of convinced and obedient Christians, the insights of the African world-view are still dominant.

And thirdly we have to reckon seriously with the conscious recovery of a neo-African culture by the intelligentzia and their considered rejection of Western systems of thought and valuation. At present this is more evident in the French-speaking territories because the *évolués* have so detested the policy of assimilation which implied that in order to be civilized they must become black Europeans. But the rejection is a reality in almost every young African intellectual today, though it may be largely repressed because he superficially accepts the Western scientific point of view and values the advantages of modern technology. Unconscious and unrecognized, his profound rejection of the Western world-view is rationalized in political terms and expressed in the tremendous drive of African nationalism. While at the moment it is being answered in political liberation it will not ultimately be satisfied in that way. More and more necessary to Africa are the spokesmen, be they poets, prophets or statesmen, who can articulate this hidden rejection of the West and, more positively, give voice to the passionate affirmations which Africa needs to make.

It is evident, therefore, that the African way of looking at things, inherent in, but also independent of, the traditional religion, stands in the world as a living faith, whether in the residual paganism of millions, or in the tacit assumptions of very many African Christians, or the neo-African culture of the intellectual leaders.

Let it be clearly understood that to say this is not to suggest that an African mind functions only according to certain peculiar thought-patterns of its own and is incapable of reasoning in a European way, as though it suffered from some innate disability. The word 'primitive', with its evolutionary overtones, has done great disservice here, and because what I have called the African way of looking at things has not found the same need as the European to discard from adult thought some of the concepts of childhood, the inference has been drawn that African attitudes are 'undeveloped'. It is significant of the advance of ethnological studies that Lucien Lévy-Bruhl, who in the early years of this century classified this way of thinking as 'pre-logical', renounced the term towards the end of his life on the sounder grounds that 'the logical structure of the human mind is the same in all men'.[1] It is not a question of capability but of culture. An African is as competent to learn and live within the complex of ideas and emphases which constitute the technological culture of 'Europe' as is a European, if he tries, to understand and enter into the African way of looking at things, or as both the African and the European, given opportunity and sympathy, are to appreciate the insights and attitudes of India or Japan. The question, How African is an African? must be answered differently, therefore, for each individual. It is theoretically possible for a young African man or woman to be quite ignorant of, and unaffected by,

[1] L. Lévy-Bruhl, *Carnets*, Paris 1949, quoted by J. Claude Bajeux in *Prêtres Noirs s'interrogent*, p. 6.

the traditional world-view; but it is much harder for the individual to know in fact whether that is so or not in his own case. All that is being posited in this study is that an African way of looking at things exists, and that it governs the values and reactions of millions, ranging from peasants to professors.

This African way is being opposed and compared, consciously or unwittingly, to the ways of the Western world, and no longer does the balance come down decisively on the side of Europe. It is through this comparison, more than in any other way, that Africans are becoming self-consciously aware of the lineaments of their culture. The rejection of Europe and the affirmation of Africa are two sides of one coin. This may take the form of the simple, figurative pronouncement of the Hausa villager, 'Europeans eat people', or the nostalgia of the sophisticated Westernized poet —

O these streets of sleeplessness, these streets of the meridians,
*   these long nightly streets!*
For so long I have been civilized and yet I have not appeased
*   the white god of sleep . . .*
But here now is my sister the breeze, that visited me in Joal,
When foreign birds sang the ancestors' message, sweet like
*   evening dew.*
The memory of your face is stretched on my throat, a
*   lordly tent,*
A vaulting of velvet that encircles the blue forest of your hair.
Your smile runs through my sky like a milky way
And the golden bees on your shady cheeks are humming like
*   stars*
And the Southern Cross is glistening on your chin.

31

And then I ejaculate a cry of carnal desire that floods my
　　heart like the Niger spreading over winter crops.
And I cry out aloud like the water to the creatures of the
　　sister trees: 'Nannyo!'
And I cry out to the couples who chatter on the honest mat
　　of the beach: 'Nannyo!'
And I shall rest a long time in blue black peace,
And I shall sleep a long time in the peace of Joal,
Until the angel of dawn returns me to your light,
To your brutal and cruel reality, civilization![1]

The rejection focuses mainly upon the European concept of individualism, upon the supremacy of the cerebral over the sensuous and intuitive ('your light, your brutal and cruel reality'), and upon the attitude of domination towards nature. An African priest speaking at a pan-Lutheran conference a few years ago, said, 'I have just read in the newspaper an article called "The Conquest of Nature". But that is absurd. If we think like that, Nature will always conquer Man.' The same critique was voiced at about the same time by a Roman Catholic priest from Ruanda: 'This mentality, founded on reason, on the scientific discipline, is directed towards the possession of the world.'[2]

While many reject Christianity with European culture, some claim that in this matter Christ stands with them rather than with Western man.

The African reading the Bible is glad to find a civilization which marches to the same rhythm as his own. No obsession

[1] Leopold Sedar Senghor, op. cit.
[2] J. Claude Bajeux, 'Mentalité noire et mentalité biblique', in *Prêtres Noirs*, p. 60.

32

with efficiency. But life as it unfolds is quite simple in its tragedy, its hopes, its slow rhythm, its cruelties too. Christ walking through the dust from one village to the next, drinking water from the wells, delighting in the movements of the sower, the radiance of the setting sun, the flowers of the field, talking at great length to the crowds – in this we find reflected the black innocence, the irresponsibility of Africa, her time-less existence, her freedom. Christ had no watch and the events of his life are rarely fastened to any date. Westerners strive to map out with some historical guide-posts the life of Christ – such is the obsession of the statisticians![1]

That avowal may be naive; yet it is impossible to deny that the elements in European culture which Africa particularly rejects are those about which many in the West also have profound misgivings. Moreover, the world Church is impoverished and incomplete without the insights that the Logos has been preparing for it in Africa. So it should be less difficult today for the representative of the universal Gospel, of whatever race, to confront the African world-view with humility and respect than it was, perhaps, when that great prophet of missionary method, Roland Allen, wrote:

We have not learnt the lesson that our own hope, our own salvation, our own glory, lies in the completeness of the Temple of the Lord. We have thought of the Temple of the Lord as complete in us. Consequently we have preached the Gospel from the point of view of the wealthy man who casts a mite into the lap of the beggar rather than from the point of view of the husbandman who casts his seed into the earth knowing that his own life and the lives of all connected with him depend upon the crop which will result from his labour.

[1] Idem, pp. 67, 68.

3

The Language of Myth

Enye tekerema na eboo nantwi nti na wanhu kasa (Twi)
The cow never learnt to speak, but not because she has no tongue

>>>◇<<<

Bᴜᴛ can the emphases of Roland Allen and, more recently, of Kenneth Cragg be applied to the Christian approach to the traditional religion of Africa or New Guinea or the Pacific Islands or the jungle tribes of India?

To put the matter in its extremest form, leaving out of account neo-Africanism and the residuum of old ideas in the Church, as the Christian meets the pagan and attempts to proclaim Christ, is it a simple case of either-or? Westermann, whose opinion cannot lightly be ignored, said yes.

However anxious a missionary may be to appreciate and to retain indigenous social and moral values, in the case of religion he has to be ruthless . . . he has to admit and even to emphasize that the religion he teaches is opposed to the existing one and the one has to cede to the other.[1]

Ruthlessness has had a long run in Africa, and so long as the missionary encounter is conceived of as a duologue one will have to 'cede to the other'. But may it not be truer to see it as a meeting of three, in which Christ has

[1] D. Westermann, *Africa and Christianity*, p. 94.

drawn together the witness who proclaims him and the other who does not know his name, so that in their slow discovery of one another each may discover more of him? It is even possible that the one who, as busy Martha, prays that her sister may be roused up to serve the Lord like herself, may learn to her surprise that that same sister has been drinking in words of his that she herself has never heard. Christ is incomparably unique. As a man in Christ the Christian shares that uniqueness; but as a man with another religion he stands in the same quest and under the same judgement as the pagan.

His desire and longing, therefore, must be to enter, sensitively and appreciatively, into that other man's world, not, first, in order to *talk* more effectively about his Lord but in order to *see* what the Lord of that world is like. Those who have not shared the terrors of a half-sinking ship at the height of a storm can never see the glory that comes walking on the waves at midnight. Only from within the nightmare world of the possessed can one know what he who casts out demons looks like, only from within the tomb can one hear the voice that summoned Lazarus, only from a cross see the dying robber's king. As Western Christians we have seen Christ coming, thank God, into our individualized lives, redeeming our particular situation, delivering us from our own type of temptation. But until our vision is aligned to the African way of looking at things, until we have felt our individuality vanishing and our pulses beating to communal rhythms and communal fears, how can we guess what that Lord looks like who is the Saviour of the African

35

world? The motive of this approach, as Walter Freytag
so often reminded us,

> . . . is much more than providing information. It is trying to
> understand. There is a great difference between them. The
> mere possession of information may involve no change at all.
> But understanding involves a two-way traffic. For you do not
> 'understand' until you have been touched (affected) yourself,
> until you get a new insight into who you are yourself. In the
> study of other religions you can amass information about their
> scriptures and doctrines. But you have not understood them
> until you have been compelled to interpret your own Gospel
> in entirely new terms. You have not really understood another
> religion until you have been tempted by the insights of this
> other religion. . . . There is no understanding of other reli-
> gions which does not yield new biblical insights. What is
> more, such understanding also yields new insights as to the
> nature of the Church.[1]

One of the first lessons that a Westerner who seeks
such understanding of Africa needs to learn is that Africans are not the direct, ingenuous children that Europeans have often pictured in contrast to the 'devious
Oriental'. On the contrary they instinctively prefer to
speak on many occasions in oblique allusions and proverbs. They adapt their thought to basic and obvious
forms of expression when dealing with people of another
race; and that is also the language of the classroom; so
boarding-school pupils often complain that when they
return to village life they can understand every word in
the conversation of the older men or women without
having the least idea what they are talking about!

[1] W. Freytag, quoted by M. A. C. Warren in *Basileia*, Evang.
Missionsverlag, Stuttgart 1959, p. 164.

The Language of Myth

The texts and cryptic mottoes on the 'mammy lorries' which provide most of the passenger transport in West Africa provide amusing examples of this oblique speech. The following are culled from a collection in Dr Margaret Field's *Search for Security*. The interpretation, added in brackets, which she got from passengers, corresponded to a remarkable degree with that volunteered by the driver-owners themselves.

'Watch and Pray.' (Because I am a prayerful and circumspect Christian I have been able to get this lorry.)

'Wages of sin is death.' (If you practise bad medicines against me you will die.)

'The beginning of life is not hard but the end.' (I got this lorry without much trouble, but shall I be able to pay for it?)

'An animal with no tail.' (From the Proverb: God looks after the animal with no tail, this means, God will help me to pay for this lorry.)

I vividly remember the first occasion on which I ventured off the beaten track of plain speaking. I wanted to talk to one of the foremost men in the village about his conviction that he had been bewitched, yet I knew that to me he could never refer directly to his sickness in any other terms than those of European medicine. Taking a proverb as my text, I launched out into a series of far-fetched, symbolic references to the forbidden topic. Not with a flicker of comprehension did he help me out, but in silence he let me flounder into ever deeper water until I ground to a standstill, certain that all communication had broken down. There was an agonizing pause. Then,

37

as it were, he came in precisely on my wavelength, using my symbolism to answer in a totally uninhibited way. It was one of the most triumphant moments I have known.

For this is a people that likes to think mythologically. There is more to be said about this in a later chapter, but here a profound quotation from Nicolas Berdyaev is apt.

Myth is a reality immeasurably greater than concept. It is high time that we stopped identifying myth with invention, with the illusions of primitive mentality, and with anything, in fact, which is essentially opposed to reality. . . . The creation of myths among peoples denotes a real spiritual life, more real indeed than that of abstract concepts and of rational thought. Myth is always concrete and expresses life better than abstract thought can do; its nature is bound up with that of symbol. Myth is the concrete recital of events and original phenomena of the spiritual life symbolized in the natural world, which has engraved itself on the language, memory, and creative energy of the people . . .; it brings two worlds together symbolically.[1]

There is an excellent illustration of this bringing together of the two worlds in a symbolism that sounds to Western ears like double-talk in Monica Wilson's richly personal study, *Communal Rituals of the Nyakyusa*.[2] The incident was reported by her husband. Kasitile, a ritual functionary and rain-maker of the aristocratic tribe that had invaded the land generations before, was frightened about recurrent sickness of various kinds from which he had been suffering. He had consulted several

[1] N. Berdyaev, *Freedom and Spirit*, Bles 1935, p. 70.
[2] Monica Wilson, *Communal Rituals of the Nyakyusa*, pp. 134–9.

diviners and suspected in turn a number of different past acts of his by which the living or the dead had been offended. For a time he had moved from the hill country to the plain in the hope of escaping whatever anger was pursuing him. Finally he had been deeply impressed by the diagnosis of another diviner who had advised him to propitiate his dead father's shade and to invite to the ceremony three village headmen, priests of the local grove, who were commoners; that is to say they were members of the aboriginal tribe which, subdued by military power, looked to witchcraft to redress the balance. So on a fixed day he called the commoner priests together with his senior kinsman and another of the chiefs' lineage, and a bull was ritually killed. Drinking and discussion continued all day in an attempt, apparently, to discover what had angered his father's shade. The crucial moments in the conversation are recorded, together with the interpretation of their significance, which Kasitile later explained to Godfrey Wilson, in brackets.

At one point Kasitile told them of the prayer he had offered at his father's shrine the previous evening, in the course of which he had said: 'Indeed, I, your wife, have done wrong. I come to enter. I am a woman.' ('So I admitted to Kissogota, the commoner priest, saying, "Indeed I have done wrong. I humble myself as your wife." ' This was Kasitile's public apology for an offence of long standing. It was now up to the commoner priests on their side to confess the hatred they had nourished against him.)

At a later stage Kasitile and Kissogota began mutual

39

compliments and self-depreciation. Kissogota said: 'You are impressive, you, you are impressive, we are only cannibals.' (This meant: 'You chiefs kill cattle for us, that is your impressiveness. Do we kill cattle? No. We eat *men*; we are witches.')

Kasitile replied: 'You are impressive yourself; if I look at you my body changes.' (This meant: 'You are impressive for you are witches. It is you who brought the chilling breath on me and said I had done wrong. If I walk about among you my body shrinks, it fears.')

After a long time Kissogota made as if to leave the company. At this one of Kasitile's companions, Mwamakunda, burst out: 'Why do you shut up words in the heart? Do you wish that Kasitile should become a fool?' (Kasitile said later of this: 'That is very important. Mwamakunda is my man, he stands by me, he eats meat with me, he compelled them to speak out, because if they do not admit that it is they then the ritual fails.')

Kissogota replied: 'We have not yet done so, Mwamakunda, we have not yet. Do you think we are angry? Who went to fetch Kasitile back from the plain? It was we, we went ourselves.'

The second commoner priest added, fiercely: 'We have power, we have. If we please we can give the chief worms.'

Kasitile and his kinsman listened without comment. It was the crucial moment to which all had led them. It was in fact the admission for which they had been made to wait so long. Kasitile later explained: 'Did not Kissogota boast? He said, "Indeed we came, it is us, it is us." He

The Language of Myth

boasted very much, he said: "We have power. If we like we can give him worms." Did I not tell you that I had worms when I came up from the plain? Where did they come from? They came from these priests, they called the shades to their aid.'

The whole process had been a ritual of reconciliation, dependent upon 'speaking out' the offence, the resulting malevolence and the fear. But it was expressed obliquely, because it had been experienced as myth, that myth which 'is a reality immeasurably greater than concept' and 'brings two worlds together symbolically'.

'It must never be forgotten' warns Dr Parrinder, 'that we have to do with a spiritual religion, however material it may appear at first sight.'[1] We shall need to remember that if we seriously intend to understand this African vision of reality, for we shall find ourselves entering a world of strange perspectives and relationships, marked with symbols that may often dismay or repel. It will be necessary to remind ourselves, for example, that if we still slaughtered our own beasts for food we would not find the details of blood sacrifice too shocking to admit of a spiritual interpretation. It is we, perhaps, who have turned over so many of the more earthy features of human life to discreetly concealed specialists, who are the unnatural ones rather than they.

Recognizing that we have to do with a spiritual religion we shall eschew much of the foreigner's terminology — 'evil spirits', 'witch-doctor', 'devil-possession' — and be constantly careful never to call another's light darkness.

[1] G. Parrinder, *African Traditional Religion*, p. 24.

The African world-view makes a clear distinction between Good and Evil; and protective charms, the detection of witchcraft, honouring and consulting the elders of the family before and after they have died, these things are to be numbered among the Good. There is evil and fear and malice enough without adding to their force by confusing good and bad.

To the African Christian such things are seen in a new light, of course. There is a sense in which a Christian, when he consults the diviner, feels that he is slipping back into darkness and is ashamed. But there was neither shame nor darkness before. Walter Freytag has a parable to meet this point.

A wood-fire can make the night bright for us. But when the sun is risen we see that its bright light makes the fire itself the cause of a shadow, so that it was not, as we supposed, pure light. What the Bible says about the religious person is in the light of the risen sun. The man who lives in the daylight cannot behave as if it were still night.[1]

Nor should Christian leaders be too anxious about the residuum of paganism within the Church. If, as we shall see, an honest meeting between Christianity and the African world-view may be creative on the frontiers of the Church, it may be even more creative within the body of the Church itself. For *de facto* it is precisely at that point of encounter and contrast and choice that the Church will get its own authentic insights into the Word. It is at the danger point, the point of interchange and temptation, that a true African theology will be born, not out of syncretism but out of understanding.

[1] W. Freytag, *The Gospel and the Religions*, SCM Press 1957, p. 39.

4

Turning Inside Out

Onipa nye abe na ne ho ahyia ne ho (Twi)
Man is no palm nut, self-contained

SOME years ago I was discussing with a friend who is a sociologist certain instances of 'spirit possession' which I had met. I admitted that in every case I had found some psychological factor – childlessness or acute anxiety – that predisposed the victim to such an attack, but I was not satisfied that the phenomenon itself could be accounted for purely subjectively. Just as shock or malnutrition might make a body more vulnerable to the disease germs which were in fact attacking all and sundry, so, I felt, psychological stress might render the personality more liable to invasion by some undefined external being or influence. My friend, on the other hand, maintained that he could not accept the objective reality of a 'something' outside, the existence of which was an unnecessary hypothesis since it must, he felt, be explained by processes inside the victim's mind. It was an inconclusive discussion and we agreed to differ. It was not until a few days after that it occurred to me that had we been looking at the question through African eyes the very alternative about which we disagreed would have ceased to exist.

Our argument hinged on the question whether the

43

causation of this phenomenon was internal or external, and we assumed that something 'outside' would have possessed an independent reality of a kind which we would not attribute to anything arising merely from the 'inside'. If anyone had asked us, inside or outside what?, we should probably have replied, the mind. Within that mysterious receptacle we locate intellect, with its endless question and answer, the coloured tapestries of imagination, the long galleries of memory, and the wisdom that emanates from them all. This is the seat of consciousness, the seat also, or is it the bed?, of the unconscious, the depository of the accumulated results of heredity and environment, training and experience. Here lie the ego and the id and the subliminal reservoirs of group consciousness and race memory. Here burn the fears and desires, the love and hate; here conscience 'hoards its strength for darkness', and guilt throbs and festers. But though these may infect the body with sickness and delude the senses with hallucinations, we believe them to be rooted within the sufferer's mind. Dreams are only dreams, for we know their fantasies are confined within the wall of the dreamer's brain.

We are in danger of forgetting that all this is only a figurative way of speaking. The spatial concepts of inside and outside cannot be used literally of something so elusive and abstract as the self; yet in Europe we have allowed them so to dominate our imagery that we have almost identified the mind with the brain and imprisoned the self within the walls of the skull.

But there have been other ways than ours of picturing

this unimaginable Self. Some philosophies, notably in the Hindu Upanishads, include on the 'inside' much that we can only imagine as being 'outside', so that even the transcendent Absolute is to be sought only within the innermost cave of the heart. But in the imagery of primal religion, on the other hand, the self is thought of as spilling out into the world beyond the confines of the experiencing body, and echoing back again from other selves. Africans would assert with St Augustine that 'we live beyond the limits of our bodies'.

One or two simple examples may clarify this other pattern of self-knowledge and help us to make the difficult effort to transpose our imaginations out of one metaphor of being and into another.

We Europeans recognize that our past experiences of people and places may have a deep and lasting effect upon our personalities. But we picture these influences as memories which we carry with us inside our minds or imaginations. Many Africans, on the other hand, seem to visualize their past experiences as operating upon them still from the external situation or event which gave rise to them. The memory of joy or pain echoes back, as it were, from the outside. I have several times noticed in Uganda that, just as parents may change the name of a child to that of an ancestor whom they think needs to be placated, so occasionally they name a child after some event in their lives as if the incident itself needs appeasing. A similar case is recorded in Godfrey Lienhardt's recent study of the religion of the Dinka. He writes:

A man who had been imprisoned in Khartoum called one of

45

his children 'Khartoum' in memory of the place, but also to turn aside any possible harmful influence of that place upon him in later life. The act is an act of exorcism, but the exorcism of what, for us, would be memories, experiences. . . . It seems that what we should call in some cases the 'memories' of experiences, and regard therefore as in some way intrinsic and interior to the remembering person and modified in their effect upon him by that interiority, appear to the Dinka as exteriorly acting upon him, as were the sources from which they derived.[1]

Exactly the same way of looking at things is revealed in a most moving poem, *The Immigrant*, by the South African writer Ezekiel Mphahlele. Self-exiled in Nigeria, where he looked to build a new life in dignity and tolerance, free from the corroding bitterness of past experience, he cannot escape the memory which reaches out after him from that land of hatred —

> *Only distant sound of long-tongued hounds*
> *I hear*
> *across the Congo and Zambesi and Limpopo*
> *down in the painful south of the south . . .*
> *Let them leave my heart alone!*[2]

As a second example we may take the simple fact that every man has a unique individuality or character. He may have a particular temperament which he cannot escape or a strong tendency to this or that which appears almost irresistible. But European thought again instinctively regards these qualities as inherent in, and inseparable from, the interior being of a person. Africans,

[1] Godfrey Lienhardt, *Divinity and Experience*, p. 149.
[2] *Black Orpheus*, Nov. 1959, Ibadan.

however, seem more inclined to argue that since these proclivities and aptitudes are things which the man experiences, they must be external to him. They are unquestionably part of his 'self', but they are separate from his 'ego'. So character is seen as a personal destiny. Meyer Fortes writes of the Tallensi of Dahomey,

Both to himself and to others the individual is what he sees himself to have achieved; and every significant achievement is credited to the goodwill of his Destiny.[1]

In Ghana it is believed that this destiny is determined by the manner in which the new living being takes leave of God before being born. It may say, 'I go to the world and like all that is agreeable, well-being, long life, all good things', or it may go forth saying, 'I choose grief, rags and dark cloth', or even 'I hate and taboo all good things and good news.' Such unsatisfactory leave-taking makes it an *okrabiri*, a black, unfortunate soul.[2] Similarly, among the Yoruba the word for destiny means 'to kneel and choose', because 'before a child is born its soul is said to kneel before the deity and choose its fate on earth. Those who humbly make reasonable requests . . . receive what they ask during their life on earth. However, those who make their requests as if they had the right to expect whatever they wanted, do not receive them.'[3]

Both Africans and Europeans, of course, are prone to

[1] Meyer Fortes, *Oedipus and Job in West African Religion*, p. 51.
[2] H. Debrunner, *Witchcraft in Ghana*, p. 12.
[3] W. R. Bascom in *American Anthropologist*, Vol. LIII.

blame fate for their failures, for there is little to choose between pre-natal destiny as an alibi or heredity and a bad home. But whereas the European thinks of his bad luck as working like a fifth column within the city of his soul, the African feels that it is an external foe, though still part of his total self. It may have to be propitiated or thanked, and the ancestors may be prevailed upon to circumvent or even change it.

A third example of this different way of looking at oneself can be seen in the universal belief that a man's brooding anger or envy very quickly can take on an existence and vitality of its own. It remains a true part of his self, yet it moves out far beyond the perimeter of his physical presence and becomes an independent agent acting back upon him as well as upon others, both living and dead. 'Anger', says an Akan proverb, 'is like a stranger, it does not stay in one house.' A man of the Lugbara tribe in north-west Uganda reported to John Middleton how this can happen when a father is justly offended by the insulting behaviour of his son:

Then this man goes home. He sits and thinks: 'if I complain at the shrines, the ghosts will do that son of mine much harm.' So he sits and thinks, but he does not say words at the shrines. But the ghosts, his father and his father's father, see him sitting and see his heart is heavy and that he wails. They think among themselves and bring sickness to that son. To say words with the mouth at the shrines is bad. If a man or an elder says words thus, his child will surely die. If he does not say words the child becomes sick and learns to obey his father, but he will not die.[1]

[1] J. Middleton, *Lugbara Religion*, p. 36.

48

Turning Inside Out

It may be noticed that there is a slight difference between this third example and the other two. They showed that some inner experience of which a man feels himself to be the object acted upon – a painful memory or an irresistible disposition – what Lienhardt terms a *passio* – is seen as an element of the self having an independent, external existence operating upon the person from whom it has derived. The last example is, rather, of an *actio*, of which the resentful father is the subject, moving out to affect first the ancestral shades and, through them, the erring son. Yet it would be wrong to make so sharp a distinction. The resentment is also a passive experience, a 'being offended', which, like the other externalized *passiones*, echoes back from outside upon the man himself as well as upon the son. That is why, in the reconciliation between Kasitile and Kissogota, recounted in the previous chapter, *both* parties had to confess their rancour, and why in that case also the ancestors themselves were caught up in the repercussions of a man's anger. 'A bad conscience and ill-will towards others', says Dr Margaret Field of the Ashanti, 'are held to disturb the peace of a man's indwelling spirit which in turn disturbs the owner's health.'[1]

Any attempt to look upon the world through African eyes must involve this adventure of the imagination whereby we abandon our image of a man whose complex identity is encased within the shell of his physical being, and allow ourselves instead to visualize a centrifugal selfhood, equally complex, interpermeating other selves in

[1] M. J. Field, *Search for Security*, p. 113.

a relationship in which subject and object are no longer distinguishable. 'I think, therefore I am' is replaced by 'I participate, therefore I am.'

African thinkers, trying to define the difference between their own and the Western view of the world put their fingers very soon on this point. Claude Bajeux writes:

Western thought has developed to their final conclusion the two principles of causality and identity. It has attempted to determine the characteristics proper to each entity, to enumerate the various relationships of which it may be the subject, to establish each entity in the place which it should occupy.[1]

In contrast to that Leopold Senghor says of African thought that

this sentient reason, the reason which comes to grips, expresses itself emotionally through the abandonment of the self in identification with its object.[2]

European writers have also pointed to this fundamental difference of outlook but have generally attributed it, unjustifiably I believe, to retarded development of the African consciousness. It is, of course, an accepted fact that in every race 'the child does not start out into life with an assured individuality, from which it sets out to conquer an outer world. It starts rather from an unresolved confusion within which the ego and the other are at first undifferentiated and out of which they are

---

[1] J. Claude Bajeux, article in *Prêtres Noirs s'interrogent*, p. 60.

[2] 'Raison sensible, *raison-étreinte*, elle s'exprime dans *l'emotion*, par l'abandon identificatrice à l'objet.' President of Senegal, Lecture at Oxford University, 26 October 1961.

developed into the comparatively sharp distinctions of adult life.'[1] So wrote Professor Grensted and went on to quote from Tennyson:

> *The baby new to earth and sky,*
> *What time his tender palm is prest*
> *Against the circle of the breast,*
> *Has never thought that 'this is I.'*
>
> *But as he grows he gathers much,*
> *And learns the use of 'I' and 'me',*
> *And finds 'I am not what I see,*
> *And other than the things I touch.'*
>
> *So rounds he to a separate mind*
> *From whence clear memory may begin,*
> *As thro' the frame that binds him in*
> *His isolation grows defined.*[2]

The same verses are quoted by Dudley Kidd in his famous *Savage Childhood* which records from his experience of Zulu children several good examples of this characteristic of very young children. He says that an African child 'will frequently beat the blanket of a person with whom he is enraged, much as a bull or an ostrich will worry the coat which a hunted man throws behind him on the ground. A child will bite its mother's blanket or petticoat in impotent rage when its will is hopelessly crossed.' He tells also how an intelligent adult Zulu recounted the first headache that he could remember in his childhood. 'He said he was conscious that something

[1] L. W. Grensted, *Psychology and God*, Longmans 1930, p. 79.
[2] Tennyson, *In Memoriam*, XLIV.

51

was wrong somewhere, but did not dream that the pain was within his head. The pain might just as well have been in the roof of his hut as in the roof of his head; and it was only when his mother told him that his head was aching that this fact dawned on him.'[1] Kidd, however, appears to ignore the fact that such incidents as these are common to small children everywhere. Presenting them as if they were peculiar to Zulu children, he proceeds to argue that this alleged inborn failure to differentiate must be the cause of the attitudes of African adults which he has noted. He says:

It takes a savage child a long time to understand all this. There seems to be a tendency in the primitive mind to assign internal or subjective agency to phenomena due to external causes, and conversely to attribute external agency to effects which are due to subjective or internal causes. When the wind moves dead leaves the adult savage is sometimes apt to think they are moved from within, and are therefore gifted with life. Conversely he thinks that sickness is often a thing sent by the ancestral spirits as though it were as frankly external as a dust-storm or pest of locusts.[2]

J. C. Carothers recognizes that infant mentality is everywhere similar, but maintains that, owing to cultural factors, it is prolonged so late in the life of the African child that its thinking never develops to the final stages of maturity. The African baby, he argues, lives in a warm secure world in continuous contact with his mother's body, he is fed whenever he demands it, his excretory activities are unrestrained. This continues with no violent break for two years or more, since weaning is

[1] D. Kidd, *Savage Childhood*, pp. 66, 61-2.   [2] Idem, p. 62.

52

very late. During this period the child never comes up against life, never counters a hard reality distinguishable from his will and appetite. 'It is not possible', says Carothers, 'to exaggerate the importance of the lengthy period of indulgence which is so characteristic of African childhood, and it is doubtless true that this must interfere, and at a critical age, with the normal human tendency to progress from unselfconscious identity with the world to objective separation.' In contrast to this, European children sleeping in their own cots, fed at regular intervals, disciplined, and then weaned early, learn by frustration to relate themselves to independent existences and wills, and develops a sense of time, an ability to contain themselves in periods of waiting, and a moderation in pleasures which patently come to an end.

After infancy, the argument goes on, children develop successively through the period of asking 'why?' to the period of asking 'how?'. Here the European child has the advantage of a variety of building blocks, balls and other toys, and a world full of mechanical appliances. These draw his attention to chains of cause and effect and the spatio-temporal relations of things and so lead him on to the maturity of being able to deduct and generalize. The African child, on the other hand, remains stuck at the stage of 'why?'; if he does progress so far as to ask 'how?', 'natural curiosity as to causes is appeased too facilely and too effectively by invocation of the super-natural, and further speculation is baulked'.[1]

[1] J. C. Carothers, *The African Mind in Health and Disease*, pp. 95–102.

The logic of this is so plausible that it invites suspicion. Kidd, for example, quotes several questions asked by young African children which reveal at least as much of a sense of selfhood as any European child might be expected to have. 'Have we changed from the people we were yesterday?', a small boy asked his mother. 'Is this body my real me?' asked another. 'What is it in me that does the thinking?', was a third question. Yet Kidd fails to see how these instances contradict his case. And in spite of the different patterns of child-care during infancy which undoubtedly have far-reaching effects, Carothers quotes S. Davidson's opinion that up to puberty there is 'very little difference in the intelligence and learning ability between Bemba and European children'.[1] The history of civilization offers, unfortunately, little evidence that man's crowning achievements in the realms of science or philosophy have depended upon four-hourly feeds or a supply of mechanical toys. That the adult African concept of selfhood has retained affinities with the consciousness of children few would deny, but it does not at all follow that this was due to an involuntary incapacity to develop beyond it.

African parents answering their children's questions unconsciously establish the impression that the question 'why?' is more important than the question 'how?'. Conceivably this is because they believe that to be true, and not only the uneducated amongst them. It was an African doctor in Uganda who said to me, 'The medical schools are very blind about sickness, they teach us only

[1] J. C. Carothers, op. cit., p. 106.

54

to ask how, but never why.' In the same way, the adult African's disinclination to draw such a sharp line as we do between subject and object does not prove that his self-awareness is undeveloped, but only that he sees no reason to discard the sense of an unenclosed, objectivized self, finding it, perhaps, truer to his experience than the myth of the mind and its contents which the European child is trained to accept. And again we should remember that there are Africans, steeped in the thought of the West, who yet feel this 'primitive' concept to be true. With that extraordinary generosity and breadth of thought that infuses all his writings Carothers himself says at the end:

No claim is made that the European approach to life is better; it is achieved at a cost. . . . It may not even be more true; the universal validity of physical determinism is a human concept and is much more evident in arm-chairs than in jungles. But this approach has tremendously increased man's power to bend the world to patterns of his choosing and is achieved by peoples whose conscious thought is governed by such principles.[1]

There he echoes Bajeux's critique: 'This mentality, founded on reason, on the scientific discipline, is directed towards the possession of the world.'

[1] Idem, p. 110.

5

The Scattered Self

Ohonam mu nni nhanoa (Twi)
The spirit of man is without boundaries

>>><<<

WE should return now to examine further how this primal view of the self operates, for it is fundamental to our understanding. We have already seen how in three instances – memory, disposition and resentment – something that we would locate 'inside' the conscious mind is regarded as operating as an external agent. The same transposition is applied to what we would call reactions of the subconscious. Africans, like ourselves, find these harder to recognize as aspects of the self, and the help of a professional is often required to 'bring them home' to a man and interpret them.

Take, for example, a guilty conscience. Lienhardt describes[1] what happens when a Dinka has failed for a long time to pay to another his cattle-debts. The creditor may not be in a position to enforce payment by a direct approach and invocation of Divinity may have been of no avail. He therefore buys a fetish. (I reserve this word to designate a parcel of magical ingredients kept in a horn or bundle, as the *locus* of a destructive power which will operate at its owner's behest, provided he maintains

[1] Godfrey Lienhardt, *Divinity and Experience*, pp. 65–6.

56

it with regular offerings.) Lienhardt says, 'This will normally involve a trip into another part of the country, or into the land of the non-Dinka peoples to the south.' People may suspect what this trip is for, but they are never quite sure. On his return the creditor will hide the fetish in his own cattle-byre, where he will visit it secretly to make offerings and speak to it. 'In return for these attentions, *mathiang gok* (the fetish) will go out after a man who owes its owner cattle. The Dinka say that it will come to such a man when he is walking alone and will speak to him and threaten to injure him or his family unless the debt is paid. It may go further, and actually kill an enemy of its owner by causing swellings.' It should be noted that swelling of the joints, 'aching all over', and wasting, are the most common psycho-somatic symptoms in Africa.

The man with whom I made my faltering debut into symbolic speech, described in chapter 3, was another debtor suffering from the visitations of a fetish. The case, which I have described elsewhere,[1] agreed in all essentials with what Lienhardt says of the Dinka. When his debility had reached a very serious point he saved himself by giving to his creditors twelve head of cattle and a furnished house, over and above the twenty acres of land he had owed them.

The fetish is unlikely to operate unless the alleged debtor is genuinely guilty; indeed it would be a bold man who dared to invoke a fetish falsely. So it is not difficult

[1] J. V. Taylor, *The Growth of the Church in Buganda*, SCM Press 1958, pp. 197–8.

to see that the power of the fetish is in fact the guilty conscience of the debtor externalized and imaged in the form of myth. Or, as Lienhardt puts it, keeping in mind his idea of the *passio*, 'the image (as we have called it) of the experience of guilty indebtedness . . . is extrapolated from the experiencing self. It comes (as memories often do) unwilled by the debtor, and is interpreted as a Power directed by the creditor.'[1]

Another of the 'contents of the mind', according to our modern Western imagery, is the group subconscious. An African prefers to think of this also as an element of his self which impinges upon him from outside. This is not the place to examine the divination of the spirit-medium, but when we do so we shall see that, however it happens, the wisdom that comes to the surface in a seance is very often the unconscious perceptions of the community, but they are voiced, in the myth, by heads of the community who have died.

A dream, also, which we picture as an eruption into the upper levels of the sleeper's mind of some of the impulses and symbolic images of the subconscious, is thought of, rather, as a real experience of one element of the self which goes forth to these encounters while other elements sleep on. This is supremely the trysting place at which the dead come to meet their living children, for, contrary to general belief, it is in Europe more than in Africa that ghosts are said to address themselves directly to the waking senses. 'My soul met with so-and-so in a dream', is a common saying in north-west Uganda,

[1] G. Lienhardt, op. cit., p. 150.

and it is immaterial whether so-and-so is from among the living or the dead. 'Dreams are different from thoughts', explained a Christian village headman in Northern Rhodesia. 'When I dream that I go to Kazembe's or to Luapula, my spirit is going there.' But as he spoke it became evident that some of those present were afraid, and a young fisherman added: 'If, after dreaming, my spirit fails to return, then I am dead.'[1]

This reference to the spirit of the dreamer brings us to the question of the constituents of the human being in African thought. If the self is so diffused that it can be both subject and object at once, what does it consist of and what are its bounds? We must beware at this point of being too precisely analytical for that would transpose the imagery back into European symbols and destroy its meaning.

In the first place the different 'relatednesses' of the self, which in the West we speak of as faculties or compartments of the mind, are pictured as separate entities rather loosely held together, each having a different source and a different function. That remains true throughout Africa, though there is a wide range between the clear specification of the different 'souls' in West Africa and the vaguer definitions of some of the Bantu tribes. As we shall see in later chapters two great elements in the living person are the power-force (Ganda – *manyi*; Ruanda – *magara*; West Africa generally – *nyama*) and the life-force (Ganda – *bulamu*; Nyakyusa – *ubumi*;

[1] J. V. Taylor and Dorothea Lehmann, *Christians of the Copperbelt*, SCM Press 1961, p. 283.

Dinka – *wei*). The latter might almost be called the life-soul. Many tribes think, as did the Hebrews, that its seat is the life-blood, that blood which the Akan believe to be inherited by every child from its mother. In West Africa the life-soul is fully personified (Twi – *kra*; Fon – *se*; Yoruba – *emi*; Nupe – *rayi*). It is given by God 'who shoots a particle of the sun's fire into the blood stream of the child thus bringing its blood to life',[1] and to God it will return at death to render account. In God's presence are the seven guardians of the days of the week, and whichever of these presents the unborn before God determines both the day on which the child shall be born and the type of life-soul that will be attached to it. Mrs Meyerowitz points out that the life-soul appears to be similar to what Freud calls the subconscious or the Id. As instinct it may save a man from danger, as impulse it is the source of his bodily and intellectual energy, as conscience it often is at war with other elements of the self and unmanned by shame or guilt. So it may be pictured sometimes as a guardian soul, the *adro* of the Lugbara people, which also returns to God at death, but to the God of the earth and of the wild.

Of greater importance is the individual-soul (General Bantu – *muzimu*; Lugbara – *orindi*; Zulu – *idhlozi*; Twi – *sunsum*; Fon – *ye*; Nupe – *kuci*) for it is this element of the

---

[1] E. Meyerowitz, 'The Concept of the Soul among the Akan', in *Africa*, XXI (1951), p. 27. Some African peoples distinguish another element in the feeling-soul (Ganda – *emmeme*; Lugbara – *asi*). This is more closely linked with physical reactions, its seat being the sternal cartilage. It is this which is disturbed in sea-sickness, and moved by beauty, sorrow or joy.

The Scattered Self

self which, after death, will live on as a shade. As such he will maintain contact with the generations that follow, expecting the filial pieties that are his due and bringing his greatly enhanced power-force to bear upon the living, either to help or to damage them. It is the individual-soul which goes forth in dreams, or even in mind-wandering, and which, as a shade, can meet the living gently in their dreams or invade their bodies violently by possession.

In several Bantu tribes there is disagreement as to whether the *muzimu* is an element in the living person. According to Jahn, there is a distinction between the living man (*muzima*) and the dead (*muzimu*). Some Baganda also say that no one is a *muzimu* until he has died. Yet this could well be a reflection of Western metaphysics, since I have heard people who supposed themselves bewitched say, 'They have attacked or taken away my *muzimu*', and one refused to be photographed lest his *muzimu* be caught in a box!

In West Africa, just as the life-soul can be likened to the Id, so the individual-soul can be identified with the conscious and distinctive Ego. Dr Parrinder calls it the personality-soul, and Dr Field says that when one man's personality dominates another's, or when an orator holds his audience spell-bound, or when a child is frozen with dismay at being caught red-handed in a theft, the individual-soul of the one is said to have seized hold of that of the other.[1]

Closely linked with the individual-soul, in the thought

[1] H. Debrunner, op. cit., pp. 14–16. The Lugbara on the other hand link personality of this sort with the transcendent-soul or *tali*.

of the Akan, is the ancestral-soul or *ntoro*, which a man inherits through his father, as he inherits his life-blood from his mother. According to Kidd, the Zulus also attach great importance to the ancestral-soul (*itongo*). As distinct from the individual-soul this is corporate. It is the ongoing life of the clan, they say. Imparted to the child by a special ceremony, it can be forfeited by a man who cuts himself off from tribal custom. After death the individual-soul may linger for a generation or so by the grave, but it is in the ancestral-soul, gathered to the fathers and living on below the homestead, that continuity endures.

We have already referred to the pre-natal Destiny which is another aspect of the self. There remains one further constituent, not greatly stressed and yet almost universally recognized, which I would call the transcendent-soul because it signifies that which a man has in common with God himself and receives directly from him. The Lugbara call it *tali*. '*Tali*' says John Middleton, 'refers to the manifestation of the power of God in his transcendent, creative, "good" aspect. . . . The *tali*, however, is not associated with man as an ancestor, as it is not associated with lineage status, and goes to dwell with God in the Sky.'[1] Among most Bantu peoples the word is *moya* or *mwoyo*, breath. The Yoruba call it *ori*, the Fon *selido*, and the Twi *honhon*. According to the last named, this is how the transcendent-soul is given. The unborn is taken into the court of the High God, Nyame, having his mother's life-blood and his father's ancestral-soul from which his own individual-soul has sprung. His

[1] J. Middleton, op. cit., p. 31.

particular day-guardian brings him before Nyame and bathes him in a golden bath. Nyame rises, utters the marching orders of Destiny, and then 'lets fall a spark-like drop of water from an *adwera*-leaf into the child's mouth. This is the water of life, *Nkwansuo*, "the pure water that boils yet does not burn". It is said to have in its centre a breathing image of Nyame, "like the figure of a person in a mirror". The water then penetrates the whole body of the child until, when filled with honhon (the breath of life) it wakes up to live.'[1]

For greater clarity we can set out the different constituents as follows:

Power-Force	Life-force
Individual-Soul	Life-soul
(afterwards the Shade)	
Ancestral-Soul	Transcendent-soul

When similar insights from different parts of Africa are collated in this way it is tempting to see a profound understanding of the complex self emerging from this grouping of linked symbols – on the one hand the father, the individuality, the conscious, the sky, the community; on the other, the mother, the blood, the earth, the wild, and the unconscious imparted by the infusion of the whole with the Spirit of God. But to do this is too clever by half. Let Western minds make their inductive and precious generalizations; Africa, if she is true to herself, remains stubbornly inarticulate. The pattern of truth is latent in the myth but it must remain immanent and

[1] H. Debrunner, op. cit., p. 11, quoting from E. Meyerowitz.

dispersed, for myth can only be analysed when it is dead or dying.

It may help us in resisting this temptation to remember that, for very many, the African self is not limited to 'souls', even in considerable numbers. A man's shadow is an extension of his self; its intensity or faintness may disclose the condition of his power-force; through it others may harm him or be blessed by him.[1] His name also is a most sensitive and powerful extension – one might almost call it a limb of the self, one which he must never put into the grip of an enemy. Possessions may also be regarded as imbued with the selfhood of their owner, particularly those, like a spear-shaft, sleeping mat or shirt, which are impregnated with perspiration or dirt from his body itself. These were the articles which were commonly buried with a man rather than his more valuable but less intimate possessions. An adolescent boy has been known to weep with shame when someone older and stronger gave his empty garments a beating.[2]

Past events which were heavily fraught with anxiety or triumph or significance for a person may have been associated with a particular object. An eland may cross a man's path on the day he is elected to a chieftainship, or he may have severed his foot with a new axe when clearing the bush. The eland or the axe will thereafter feature centrally in his memory of the event; he will feel that he has a special relationship with them. In an earlier instance we saw how a father exorcised the impact of his externalized memory by placating the name Khartoum.

[1] Cp. Acts 5.15.   [2] D. Kidd, op. cit., pp. 66–8.

64

The Scattered Self

Had there been a visible object instead of a name associated with the unhappy memory he might have placated that instead. So, in these other examples, the eland
or the axe may become emblems of a permanent external
influence working upon him and demanding his reverence. This is the origin of totemism, and many of the
clan totems of Africa, like the heraldic emblems of
Europe, are the relics of some forgotten event in the life
of an ancestral head, whose self, with the self of the
whole clan, is extended into, and lives on in, the totem.

Perhaps there are few things more important for the
Western Christian in Africa, or, for that matter, for the
African Christian as well, than to enter into this vision
of selfhood and to appreciate its validity. For the Gospel
is for men as they are and as they think they are, and this
is the self that is potentially the New Man in Christ. What
has the Christian, present in such a world, to share or to
learn about the self? He believes, to quote Dr J. H. Old-
ham, that

the isolated individual self is an abstraction. We become persons only in and through our relations with other persons.
The individual self has no independent existence which gives
it the power to enter into relationships with other selves.
Only through living intercourse with other selves can it
become a self at all.[1]

On the face of it, that seems more congenial to Africa
than to Europe. But Christ is never congenial anywhere,
or he would not be Christ. For he asserts that the way into
life is the way of the death of self, and that, God knows,

[1] *The Times*, 5 October 1933.

is best taught not by speaking but by dying. But here's the rub. What does death-of-self mean for a self that is dispersed into many centres of consciousness far beyond the narrow circle of the skull and the precincts of the flesh? Asceticism is too introverted and confined, so is the self-surrender of the isolated soul. Perhaps a hint of what death of this African self must mean is to be found in the tantalizingly sketchy outline of the work that Dietrich Bonhoeffer was not spared to write, the brief notes of which represent the last record of his thought. Among them are these words:

Encounter with Jesus Christ. Experience that here we have a reversal of all human being, in the fact that Jesus exists only for other people . . . not in the Greek divine human form of 'man in himself', but 'the man for others!'[1]

For the time being that must remain no more than a clue, for we are only at the start of this venture into understanding.

[1] Dietrich Bonhoeffer, *Letters and Papers from Prison*, SCM Press 1953, p. 179, but I have used the translation by James Mark from an article in *Prism*, VI, 2 (1962), p. 61.

6

The Unbroken Circle

Nsem nyinaa ne Nyame (Twi)
The All-Thing is God

>>>◇<<<

O n one occasion I spent the whole night working with
a team of roving fishermen on Lake Victoria. I arrived
at the grassy space on the shore where the canoes were
drawn up to find the men still asleep in their huts. So I
spent an hour under a tree, chatting to three urchins,
typically tough little harbour rats, and watching the
brown hawks and startlingly white egrets swooping round
the refuse by the canoes, while a great fish eagle cruised
lazily high above the lake. The long nets hung from a
trellis in the sun; behind them water and sky were a
brilliant blue. Slowly the camp came to life. Three or
four of the men began tying stones wrapped in banana
fibre as fresh weights along the lower edge of the nets.
Then the nets were rolled and placed in the canoe.
Meanwhile the women – the casual companions who
agreed to live with the men during the months of
their stay in this place – were stowing the mats and
blankets and a cooking pot of peeled plantains. There was
a long delay while someone cycled off to buy a bottle of
paraffin for the lamp, but by six o'clock we were away,
ten of us paddling in pairs, a steersman with a heavier

paddle at the stern, and one of the harbour rats to bale.

The lake turned to fire as the sun went down and above the shadowed shores the hills stood out bathed in brighter light. The men were silent, making up the lost time. All together they raised their spear-shaped paddles, the arm that gripped the butt lifted straight above their heads, the other hand grasping halfway down the shaft. So they poised. Then in unison came the downward stab, the rasping of the shafts along the edge, the flash of wet blades breaking surface and the arms thrust upwards again, on and on. Their unrelenting endurance dismayed me. The muscular pain grew nearly intolerable, and I was alone in it. Somehow I kept the stroke, but in every way I was odd man out, violent and clumsy. I wished I had stayed at home. The men were singing now, led by the steersman. On the seat in front of me a boy of thirteen stopped once to take off his bright green shirt but apart from that he never faltered. I could see the ripple of his muscles under the sheen of his back, and his slender arm raised like a gesture of defiance before each fierce thrust into the water. Suddenly I was no longer an individual struggling to keep in time. The rhythm had caught me. Then there was the steady burning ache but no more tiredness or need to stop.

We swept on down the bay, passing one forested finger of land after another. In the lee of the last headland of the bay we rested for a few minutes. The opposite arm, curving to meet us, was just visible in the fading light. Above us rode a crescent moon, with the evening star, 'the Moon's wife', glowing just below it.

The Unbroken Circle

As we left the shelter of the bay for the open lake the wind pounced and soon we were bobbing like a cork in a turmoil of waves. Excitement rose high and all paddled as if it were a battle, spearing down at the old enemy that threatened them. Again and again a long white breaker racing towards us seemed as if it must curl over into the boat and swamp us, but the steersman wrenched us round to take it diagonally so that we never shipped more than a few gallons. Yet for all his skill it looked as if our narrow sliver of wood could not long survive in such a sea. It was a unison of fear that held us now, and yet not only fear. For in a quite indescribable way the power and exultation of the waves was in us too and the wind was singing with us. They pointed at each hissing line of foam charging towards us and roared with laughter as the wave swept under us and we plunged into the trough on the other side.

As we turned to run parallel to the shore we reached quieter water, though the wind was still strong. Somewhere along the coast to our left was the shrine of the divinity Kokola which I had visited some weeks before. Looking out over the lake was a series of caves cut in two tiers into the face of an overhanging cliff, their mouths veiled with a curtain of lianas trailing from the forest above. I had seen the lower caves filled with the property of the roving fishermen – bicycles, nets, paddles, and tins containing cash – left there while the owners visited their homes in Tanganyika, unguarded save by Kokola himself. Our steersman had told me that there is no thief, however irreligious, who will dare to steal things left in

69

the keeping of this divinity, for those who have attempted it have always been struck dead.

We beached on a tiny cove of silver sand at the foot of a black mass of forest trees. The wind was too strong for fishing and for a while the men stood around with their shirts flapping discussing what should be done. Five went to gather firewood while the rest of us rolled in our blankets on the sand, our feet almost in the water, to snatch some sleep. After an hour the wind had dropped and the leader went from one swathed figure to the next shaking us awake. I found a fire had been lit at the foot of a giant *nkoba* tree, and four men were pushing off in the canoe into the dark. The rest of us sat talking round the lamp in low, sleepy voices. Out of sight the boat was making a wide semi-circle guided by the lamp on the shore, while the man at the prow steadily paid out first the rope and then the long net with its line of bobbing corks. At last we heard them beaching forty yards away to our right.

Then began the long haul, four men to each rope at opposite ends of the little cove. Slowly at first we started dragging the ropes in from the lake. The young boy, squatting where the sand met the edge of the forest, coiled the rope as our four drew it up the beach towards him. Soon the drag of the wet rope became heavier. As each of us reached the boy he let go, walked back to the water's edge and took his place again in the endless tug of war – haul up, walk down, to and fro, the rope burning in our grip and drawing a cool line of wetness across our shoulder blades. One man, passing me on his

70

The Unbroken Circle

way down to the water rubbed a hand over his sore shoulders. 'We have the same pain', I murmured to him. 'And one power', he grunted, clutching the rope again behind me. For the second time I felt the edges of separateness evaporating.

At last the word was given to converge and draw together the two ends of the net that were just coming to shore. Slowly the great circle was drawn tighter, men wading out to hold its wall upright. Soon we could hear the hiss of the churned up water at the apex where all the fish were crowding, then we could see the foaming silver, and the last yards of net, like a great bag, were heaved through the shallows to the dry sand.

Three times we dragged. Then we made towards the fire for supper, and sat in a circle under the inky trees. Tin plates were handed round, each with a whole boiled fish upon it, and in the centre was a great basket of steamed plantain. As I reached my arm towards it a firm hand restrained me. I looked up to see every head bowed, as together they intoned a long Latin grace.

To whom was this incongruous incantation? To the God of the Absolutes, who seemed as remote from us then as the sonorous phrases of that dead and alien tongue? To the dark forest, or some genius of the place like Kokola? Or perhaps to that unison of all being which I had twice been made aware of that night? I learned later that all except the young boy were from the same village in Tanganyika which lies in the orbit of a Catholic Mission. But that did not answer my question.

I have recounted this experience at some length be-

71

cause, though highly subjective, it may help to make significant to the imagination something of that sense of cosmic oneness which is an essential feature of primal religion. Not only is there less separation between subject and object, between self and not-self, but fundamentally all things share the same nature and the same interaction one upon another – rocks and forest trees, beasts and serpents, the power of wind and waves upon a ship, the power of a drum over a dancer's body, the power in the mysterious caves of Kokola, the living, the dead and the first ancestors, from the stone to the divinities a hierarchy of power but not of being, for all are one, all are here, all are now. This experience of the world is not limited to the simple peasant. It permeates the consciousness of African thinkers and writers even after long acquaintance with the Western world. The poet who writes,

I saw the sky in the evening snow cotton flowers and
seraphims' wings and sorcerers' plumes,

is speaking out of a mystical awareness of the actual affinity of things which survives amongst us only as metaphor or in the studied effects of surrealism. No distinction can be made between sacred and secular, between natural and supernatural, for Nature, Man and the Unseen are inseparably involved in one another in a total community.

Something of this awareness is expressed and, perhaps, accounted for in the Bushmen's myth of creation as retold in Laurens van der Post's *The Heart of the Hunter*.

The Unbroken Circle

The story comes from that group of Bushmen whose name for the Spirit of Creation is *Dxui*, known as *Tsui* or *Tuiquo* by the Hottentots, and transferred to the Xhosa and Pondo as *Thixo*.[1]

When the sun rose Dxui was a flower. The birds ate of him as a flower until the sun set. The night fell. He lay down and slept. The place was dark and the sun rose. Dxui tall as a tree was another and larger kind of flower, but when the night fell Dxui was Dxui. The sun rose and Dxui again was a flower – a light-coloured flower that turned into a green fruit which ripened red in time, but when the sun went down again Dxui was a man who rested. When the sun rose again, Dxui was Dxui and went away to become a palm. . . .[2]

So through one metamorphosis after another the tale unfolds, not of a divine *making*, for, inconsequently, birds, sun and so on were already there, but of a divine *involvement*. It is the immanence that creates the underlying unity of all things. There is a West African myth that when God withdrew from the world he entrusted it to a power called *bunsi* or *mkissi-nsi*, the world-energy. This is the power-force already mentioned in the last chapter. It is the central principle of the primal world-view, best known to the West under the Melanesian name of *Mana*. It is an all-pervasive potency in every element and every creature, present in man and present with a greatly enhanced intensity in the dead. What Father Placide Tempels says of the Bantu is equally true of the Sudanic Negroes of West Africa, that they

[1] The letter 'x' in such names represents a 'click' which some European writers have approximated with a 'qu-'.
[2] Laurens van der Post, *The Heart of the Hunter*, p. 152.

. . . cannot conceive a man as an individual existing by himself, unrelated to the animate and inanimate forces surrounding him. It is not sufficient to say he is a social being; he feels himself a vital force in actual intimate and permanent *rapport* with other forces – a vital force both influenced by and influencing them.[1]

Man in his weakness, confronting the implacable forces of nature and the thousand dangers lurking, he knows not where, in ambush, craves this power to supplement his incapacity. So

the supreme happiness, the only kind of good fortune is for the Bantu the possession of the fullest vital potency. The worst adversity and, indeed, the only kind of misfortune is for him the diminution of this power. Every sickness, affliction or adversity, each injustice and every frustration is all regarded and described by the Bantu as a diminution of the vital force.[2]

But if his resources of potency are abundant then he will describe his condition in words similar to Job's: My glory is fresh in me, and my bow is renewed in my hand. This happiness is not to be sought through a rapacious individual grasping of the power-force latent in other beings. That way lies witchcraft. A man's well-being consists, rather, in keeping in harmony with the cosmic totality. When things go well with him he knows he is at peace, and of a piece, with the scheme of things, and there can be no greater good than that. If things go wrong then

[1] Placide Tempels, *Bantoe-Filosofie*, Antwerp, 1946, p. 30.
[2] Tempels, 'La Philosophie Bantoue', *Présence Africaine*, 1949, p. 34.

The Unbroken Circle

somewhere he has fallen out of step. He feels lost. The totality has become hostile and, if he has a run of bad luck he falls a prey to acute insecurity and anxiety. The whole system of divination exists to help him discover the point at which the harmony has been broken and how it may be restored.

In this primal view, man's position vis-à-vis the world, therefore, is not one of exploitation but of relationship. This does not mean that the African regard for nature is that of romanticism or of reverence for life. Peasants in Africa are both as tender and as insensible in their treatment of other living things as peasants anywhere else. There is often brutality in what they do, and in what they suffer, but always the relationship is essentially personal.

> *Hear more often things than beings,*
> *the voice of the fire listening,*
> *hear the voice of the water,*
> *Hear in the wind*
> *the bushes sobbing,*
> *it is the sigh of our forebears.*

But at this point there is a divergence. Man has found two ways of interpreting this sense of presence which confronts him in the world. One is that which appears to have been general in the ancient Semitic religions and is found in some manifestations of primal religion today:

Nature is alive, and its powers are distinguished as personal because man has directly experienced them. There is no such thing as the inanimate. Man lives in the realm of a throbbing, personal nature, the kingdom of the holy gods. He is caught

75

in the interplay of gigantic forces to which he must integrate his life. They are known to him because he has experienced them, not as objects but as personalities so much greater in power than his own that of necessity he worships and serves them.[1]

But in Africa the worship of the forces of nature, or of free nature spirits that are not of human origin, is rare. The Bushmen and the Hottentots adore sun and moon, the morning star and the southern cross, but only as symbols of divinity. The first missionary to Africa of the modern era, George Schmidt, reported how the Hottentots, whom he reached in 1737, celebrated the return of the Pleiades.

As soon as these stars appear above the eastern horizon mothers will lift their little ones on their arms, and running up to elevated spots will show to them these friendly stars, and teach them to stretch their little hands towards them. The people of the Kraal will assemble to dance and sing according to the old custom of their ancestors. The chorus always sings: O *Tuiqua*, our Father above our heads, give rain to us.[2]

The Bushmen and the Ngombe of northern Congo regarded the waning and waxing moon as the symbol and origin of death and renewal. Several Bantu tribes used to observe a 'sabbath' of the new moon. Something more like a positive cult exists in some places for an Earth Goddess. As *Masala* in the southern Nubian mountains

[1] G. Ernest Wright, *The Old Testament against its Environment*, SCM Press 1950, p. 17.
[2] Theophilus Hahn, *Tsuni-Goam, the Supreme Being of the Khoi-Khoi*, Routledge and Kegan Paul 1881, p. 43.

she stands alone, but in West Africa she is regarded as
the consort, or opposite principle, to the Sky God. She is
the Demeter or Great Mother, and also the recipient of
the dead. The Kono and the Temne peoples of Sierra
Leone usually begin prayers with the words, 'Great God,
and Chief of the Earth (*Dugbo*), and you ancestral Elders,
help me.' *Asase Yaa*, the Thursday Earth Mother of the
Akan, is similarly always linked with the High God, as
is the earth goddess of the Yoruba whose worship, stem-
ming from the aboriginal culture, is kept alive by the
Ogboni secret society. The Yoruba pantheon has divinities of storm and thunder, of the ocean, the Niger and
other rivers. The *Balubaale* of the Baganda include lords
of earth and death, of rainbow, lightning and plague.

It could be that all of these represent an earlier, ani-
mistic stage in African religion before the great tribal
ancestors and hero-gods took pride of place. But the evidence does not point that way. It seems, rather, that
these nature-divinities also are essentially human heroes
whose power has become identified with that of a particular natural phenomenon that was at one time associated
with them. *Ogun*, for example, the Yoruba warrior who
by the use of iron weapons conquered the aboriginal city
of Ire in Ekiti, has become the blacksmith's 'god of war'
and the tutelary deity of mechanics and lorry drivers.
We have also seen already how the totems of families and
the clan divinities such as the *misambwa* of the Ganda,
the *yeeth wun* of the Dinka or the *mandwa* in Rwanda,
originated, probably, as emblems associated with ancestral figures which have become the living symbols and

77

vehicles of the continuing self and generative power of
the clan. Many tribes think of certain snakes appearing
in their houses or plantations as embodiments of particular ancestors – they do not worship snakes as such.
They may venerate a stream as the 'child' or embodiment
of a woman that died at its source – the stream is not a
goddess. Trees, mountains, rocks are reverenced and
feared, but only as the abode of spirits that were human.
Nature worship is not characteristic of Africa in the sense
that natural objects are peopled with non-human spirits.
Nature is personal because she is the medium in which
human personality and will is continually operating.

For, though an African 'feels himself a vital force in
actual, intimate and permanent *rapport* with other forces',
he recognizes a uniqueness in the force that is human.
The Suto say to their children: *u se ke ua ba ntho, u be
motho* – don't be a thing, be a person. Human means not
only all living men, but the dead also and the great
ancestors and hero-gods, all of which, in the Bantu lan-
guages, share a noun-class of their own. And the uniqueness of the human force lies in its possession of creative
intelligence and will which can directly strengthen or
weaken another human in his life-force; can influence
the force of non-human things; can control the force of a
thing to influence the life force of another person. This
creative intelligence releasing the force in things is the
principle underlying the use of herbal medicines and
magic, the arts of the safety-doctor and the powers of the
witch. But it also operates in every creative activity of
man. Janheinz Jahn writes:

78

The Unbroken Circle

Sowing alone is not sufficient to make the maize germinate and grow; speech and song must be added, for it is the word that makes the grasses germinate, the fruits grow, the cow go in calf and give milk. Even handicrafts need the word if they are to succeed.

And he quotes Senghor:

The prayer, or rather the poem that the goldsmith recites, the hymn of praise sung by the sorcerer while the goldsmith is working the gold, the dance of the smith at the close of the operation, it is all this – poem, song, dance – which, in addition to the movement of the artisan, completes the work and makes it a masterpiece.[1]

But in this personalized universe, where all that happens happens through the working of the creative intelligence of some 'human' agency, everything becomes arbitrary. Westernized men, having surrendered to the scientist the task of explaining the phenomena of his life, is prepared to take a great deal for granted. Assuming a mechanistic causation in every event he can afford to let a multitude of incidents pass as accidental with no sense of insecurity or of wonder. But for the man who assumes a personal causation in every event there is no such thing as accident. Any occurrence may be significant for his well-being and therefore needs to be accounted for in terms of some personal will, either of the living or the dead. Life becomes an unceasing Who-goes-there?, and a man alternates between triumph and anxiety. For this creative intelligence of human kind is weakest in living men, and there is little they can do unless it is supple-

[1] Janheinz Jahn, *Muntu*, Faber 1961, pp. 125, 126.

mented from the vastly greater resources of the dead and the hero-gods. For there is a hierarchy of the all-pervasive power force. Edwin Smith, interpreting Father Tempels, says:

Above all forces is God, who gives existence and increase to all others. After him come the first fathers, founders of the various clans, who form links in the chain binding God and man. . . . Next to them come the so-called 'dead' of the tribe who are other links in the chain – or, say, channels through which the vital force influences the living generation. The 'living' in their turn form a hierarchy according to their vital power. The eldest of a group or clan is the link between the ancestors and their descendants. The chief, duly appointed and installed according to traditional rules, reinforces the life of his people and all inferior forces, animal, vegetable and organic. . . . Inferior to the human forces are those resident in animals, plants and minerals.[1]

It is difficult for the Western mind, trained to see distinctions and antitheses, to grasp how all-inclusive and self-sufficient is this African world. Is there no dualism to break its homogeneity? There seem, certainly, to be a few glimpses here and there of a balance of mighty opposites. We have seen already how the powers of sky and earth are regarded as consorts. The Lugbara contrast God in his immanence, the manifestation of the wild that lies beyond the edges of cultivation, and God transcendent above and beyond the world, the source of life and health. The Dinka deepen this contrast in their belief in *Macardit* the Outsider, who presides over the inexplicable injustices of life and 'the inevitable and sometimes

[1] Edwin W. Smith, in *African Ideas of God*, p. 18.

80

brutal curtailment of human life and fertility'.[1] This opposition is reflected among living men in the difference between the practice of safety medicine and the practice of witchcraft, and among the shades in the difference between ordinary parental spirits and the restless ghosts of those who at their death carried their envy or malice with them. The most complete antithesis is that between the High God and the Adversary, such as the Akan *Nyankopon Kweku* or the *Rwuba* of Rwanda, who, essentially evil, is always planning to spoil what God is doing. The Vugusu of Kavirondo ascribe all evil things to 'the black god' who is working against *Wele Xakaba*, God the Great Giver. This is typical of their prayers to God –

> Wele, *you who made us walk in your country*,
> *You who made the cattle and the things that are in it*,
> *Drive away the black god*,
> *He may leave your man*,
> *He may move into the snake*
> *And into the abandoned homestead*,
> *He may leave our house.*[2]

Yet even these contraries are embraced within the monistic totality. 'They are not', says Lienhardt, 'conceived as "beings" actively pitted against each other, as experiences in themselves cannot actively oppose each other. The difference between them is not intrinsically in them but in the human experiences they image.'[3] Africa, like the author of Ecclesiastes, meets life's tragic contrariety not with the battle-cries of dualism but the

[1] Godfrey Lienhardt, *Divinity and Experience*, pp. 81, 83.
[2] *African Worlds*, ed. Daryll Forde, p. 44.
[3] G. Lienhardt, op. cit., p. 159.

tolerant shrug of agnosticism. The Mende of Sierra Leone call God, He-who-gives-and-rots. '*Imana* who sends famine', say the Banyarwanda, 'also provides a place to buy food.' The Akan have a more bitter proverb: 'The Manifold Lord created Death and Death killed Him.' And the Dinka sing –

> *Spring rain in a dry spell, strikes the ants on the head*
> *   with a club*
> *And the ants say: My father has seen*
> *And they do not know whether he helps people*
> *And they do not know whether he injures people.*[1]

Is this *deus incertus* all that the rounded circle of existence contains of God? That is the question to which we must now turn.

[1] G. Lienhardt, op. cit., p. 55.

Oh That I Might Find Him!

Enhombo hadi ombo omuti umue ne Pamba (Ambo)
The cattle shelter under the same tree with God

ETHNOLOGISTS have not yet been able to agree as to
what place God occupies in the African world-view.
Some argue strongly that Africans have always believed
in a High God while others contend that there was no
place for such a God, and no hint of him in the traditional ritual. But few seem to have fastened upon the significance of this ambivalence. Both views are true, and the
inability to reconcile them is central to primal religion.

On the one hand I find it impossible to dispute a universal recognition of, and desire for, the Ultimate God.
The proof for this seems to lie not so much in the titles
of the Creator which are used today in every tribe, for
these may reflect an imported teaching, but rather in the
references everywhere in songs and proverbs and riddles,
whose archaic grammatical forms attest their antiquity.
These reveal the deep sense of a pervading Presence –
'The cattle shelter under the same tree with God.'
'Wherever the elands graze in herds, there is God.' 'God
is in the great trunk and in the low branches.' 'If you
would tell God, tell it to the wind.' 'God is in front: he
is in the back.' His praise-names, rather than the actual

proper names now used, often reveal the same concept – 'He who is met everywhere'; 'Ocean with horizon head-band'; 'Infinity of the Forest'; 'He who fills all'; and the ancient farewell greetings 'Go with God': 'Stay with God'.

But while everywhere there seems to be an underlying conviction that such a God *is*, it is accompanied, and usually overwhelmed, by the pragmatic knowledge that such a God has gone away. The African myth does not tell of men driven from Paradise, but of God disappearing from the world. It is man, not God, whose voice calls through the desolate garden, Where art thou?

> *Hush, child of my mother*, croons the Burundi lullaby –
> *Hush, hush, O my mother!*
> *Imana, who gave you to me,*
> *If only I could meet him*
> *I would fall on my knees and pray to him.*[1]

'So because men had done wrong, God withdrew himself into heaven.' From every part of the continent the story is told in those terms. Man projects his inward sense of the lost Presence and fixes God in the sky. The pervasive Spirit becomes the remote and unknowable Creator, the First Cause, the Owner. The more recent names for the Deity almost always convey this meaning – Lord of the Sky, Moulder, Great Chief. And, paradoxically, this transcendent God is the one that, in Africa, man has made in his own image.

The Yoruba have a significant word for worship, *she orisha*, which means 'to make the God'. One who has closely studied the traditional cults of Nigeria goes so far

[1] Rosemary Guillebaud in *African Ideas of God*, p. 197.

as to say that the god exists through his worshippers. He is believed to live in anyone who has once been possessed by him. It is generally recognized that the personality of the worshipper is changed and will thereafter embody the spiritual ideals represented by that god. But equally the popular conception of the god's personality is modified by the traits of character and behaviour exhibited by some devotee whose personality makes its mark upon the history of the cult.

Man's worship not only delineates the features of such gods, but raises their status higher and higher. Beginning in this world as part of the 'human' hierarchy of the living and the ancestors, they are eventually, as we might say, pushed through the sky-light and lost sight of. In her study of the changes that Nyakyusa religion has undergone during twenty years, Monica Wilson has given a vivid account of how this may take place.[1] The Nyakyusa look back to three 'founding fathers', *Nkekete*, *Kyala* and *Lwembe*, who migrated from a mountain range to the east some four hundred years ago, bringing with them cattle and new types of crops and also the knowledge of fire and the smelting of iron. *Nkekete* and *Kyala* were both killed, while still childless, one at a rocky pool, the second in a cave; *Lwembe* founded the aristocratic dynasty. These three were soon looked upon as the guarantors and preservers of fertility, as were the sacred kings and the chief's lineage, the 'lords', who were the heirs of *Lwembe*. All three heroes were reverenced with prayer and sacrifice. But *Kyala* who never had living

[1] Monica Wilson, *Communal Rituals of the Nyakyusa*, pp. 2–18.

heirs, had no priest-representatives in the succeeding generations. By 1935 *Kyala* was being worshipped at his cave for his creative power, but he was still one of the hero-gods, dwelling 'beneath' with the shades, as opposed to 'above', in the sense of 'on earth'. There was no hint of a sky-God nor of one single supreme power. But in 1955 the apotheosis of *Kyala* was complete. He had come to be the ultimate power and first cause, unique and omnipotent; now his dwelling place was 'above', in the sense of 'in the sky' as opposed to 'below', i.e. 'on earth'. And by the same token he had become remote, blamed for all that is incomprehensible in life, and therefore more and more ignored in practical affairs. For, says Mrs Wilson, 'men are preoccupied with their relationships to other living men – their kinsmen, neighbours and fellow office-holders – and with their dead fathers. They are not concerned with their relationship to *Kyala*. The rituals celebrated by kinsmen are directed to the shades, not to any Supreme God.'[1]

Among the Nupe of Northern Nigeria 'the most common and most strongly emphasised comment on the nature of the deity is *Soko lokpa*, God is far away, yet in a different, more mystic sense he is present always and everywhere'.[2] This is the dichotomy in primal religion. The intimate Presence which is the form in which God belongs to the African world-view has been hidden by man's inner estrangement; the God who is 'Outside', whom African man has 'made', is too remote to meet

[1] Monica Wilson, *Communal Rituals of the Nyakyusa,*, p. 164.
[2] S. F. Nadel, *Nupe Religion*, p. 11.

man's needs. So God, says Miss Guillebaud, 'does not enter into daily life at all, in a practical sense, and yet he is continually in the people's thoughts'.[1] Caught between the two interpretations of God, the Dinka sing

Great Deng is near, and some say 'far'
    O Divinity
The creator is near, and some say 'he has not reached us'
    Do you not hear, O Divinity?
The black bull of the rain has been released from the moon's
        byre
    Do you not hear O Divinity?[2]

There are a few African tribes – the Ashanti, the Dogon, the Ambo and perhaps three or four more – in which the Supreme God was actively worshipped in the traditional religion with a cult and a priesthood; but in the great majority no shrines are raised to him and no sacrifices offered. People may pray to him still in moments of special personal need, as Hannah prayed at Shiloh once:

I prostrate myself before you, Imana of Burundi, I cry to you: give me offspring, give me as you give to others! Imana, what shall I do, where shall I go? I am in distress, where is there room for me? O merciful, O Imana of mercy, help this once.

Margaret Field reports a moving incident at a household where mourning was being made for a boy who had died and the ancestral shades were being invoked. As she stood in the courtyard in the dark she suddenly became aware that the father had stepped outside to the back of the hut and was standing alone with his head pressed

---

[1] Rosemary Guillebaud, art. cit., p. 186.
[2] Godfrey Lienhardt, op. cit., p. 38.

against the wall, weeping, and saying, 'O Father, God, why have you done this?'

There is more direct prayer to the High God in West Africa but usually among the Bantu men only turn to him as a last resort when the ancestors and hero-gods have failed. The leader of a hunting expedition in Nyasaland which had had no luck for two weeks, exclaimed, 'I am tired of asking the shades, let us pray to God.' Some say that the ancestors and hero-gods are only the intermediaries who act as the junior chiefs in the hierarchy and carry men's requests to God; but the fact is men are doubtful whether their affairs are the proper concern of so high a deity even if they could command his attention. 'Complaints and wishes are not directed to the world-order itself, a woman who pleads to have a child does not want any change in the fundamental laws of the cosmos. With one's personal cares and wishes one turns to the ancestors.'[1]

The Christian, with his theology grounded in the doctrine of the transcendence must pass through an agonizing abnegation if he is to understand imaginatively how essentially this-worldly is the closed circle of being which is the African world, and how little it needs a transcendent God. 'The sky is immense,' says the Yoruba oracle, 'but it grows no grass'. Cullen Young says:

When the New Testament enters Africa it comes up against a system of thought – and therefore into contact with habits of life – based upon the theory of the eternal self-sufficiency of the clan.... Under the communal bond heaven in the

[1] Janheinz Jahn, *Muntu*, p. 115.

sense of an after-life is assured to the clansman. It is a clan heaven to which he, or she, goes without fail provided that in life no act has been committed which would involve exclusion from the clan. It is the continuing habitation of one's own folk and . . . there is actually no place for God.

For, as he goes on to explain,

that view of life that retains the ancestors within the clan as Elder Statesmen gives 'the Owner' no place in the clan heaven.[1]

Hitherto in this encounter Christianity, like Islam, has been essentially the champion and the herald of the transcendent God. Undoubtedly it was the influence of the missions, and their adoption of this or that name to designate the God of the Bible, which helped to crystallize the concept of a supreme Creator even among those who did not become Christians. Let us never underestimate the magnitude of this revelation. The Gospel adds dimensions of grace to the image of transcendence which the wit of man could never have devised. The offer is made that all who were far off can be made nigh. The Creator is revealed as Father, the Great Ancestor of a larger clan that is to embrace and supersede all lesser tribes. And, in Christ, he who is above and beyond is shown to have broken into the closed circle to become one with men.

All that has been most faithfully proclaimed and faithfully believed, even to martyrdom. And yet too often the dichotomy has remained unbridged. The Incarnation has been presented as an isolated crossing over rather than as the closing of the gulf. The Christian's God is called

[1] T. C. Young, *African Ways and Wisdom*, pp. 24–5, 44.

Father but to the majority this signifies only that he is creator and supreme head. His name occurs far more than of old in prayers and in curses; but the shrug of cynical practicality continues. Such was the response to the Gospel of one group of islanders on Lake Victoria: 'My fire is my God, for it cooks the food I eat.' 'Our God is our food and our pipes, nothing else.' 'I know God, he made all things, but I don't want to worship him, you can teach the children.' Such, fundamentally, is still the response of many Christians of the second and third generation, who find that any High God is too separated from the world and turn, in an emergency, to the diviners and safety-doctors and parental shades which their fathers trusted. God, in spite of grace, has not been brought inside. Now Africa's century of acquiescence is coming to an end and the old views and values are reasserting themselves. If God remains 'outside' much longer, Africa's this-worldliness will turn to materialism.

Perhaps it was my half-aware glimpses of these things through African eyes that made the closing pages of Bonhoeffer's book, which I have already mentioned, such a revelation to me. He might, in a strange way, almost have been describing that earth-centred, self-contained totality when he wrote:

God is teaching us that we must live as men who can get along very well without him. The God who is with us is the God who forsakes us. The God who makes us live in this world without using him as a working hypothesis is the God before whom we are ever standing.[1]

[1] Dietrich Bonhoeffer, *Letters and Papers from Prison*, p. 164.

Oh That I Might Find Him!

What, then, would this man who understood with such sympathy the impossibility of 'religion' in the world that is all here and all now, have to say of the God of the Absolutes?

What is God? Not in the first instance a general belief in God, in God's omnipotence etc. That is no genuine experience of God but a bit of extended world. Encounter with Jesus Christ. Experience that here we have a reversal of all human being, in the fact that Jesus exists only for other people! The existence-for-other-people of Jesus is the experience of transcendence! Omnipotence, omniscience, omnipresence, spring from freedom from oneself, from existence for others unto death. ... Our relationship to God is not a 'religious' one to the highest, most powerful, best being conceivable – that is not transcendence – but our relationship to God is a new life in 'existence for others', in participation in the being of Jesus.[1]

That, strangely enough, is the God of the Bushman's dream with which we began. For after becoming the many kinds of flowers, *Dxui* became 'a new kind of tree – a tree with a difference since although it bore fruit it was also covered with thorns – the first emblem of worldly rejection and inner loneliness'. The woman appears then and tries to possess the fruit of the tree which is *Dxui*. But that cannot be, and *Dxui* vanishes, and the woman, weeping, dies. Thence, from a new beginning, *Dxui* became many new creatures in turn, always with an intenser hunger for being, until, as a man, he was rejected and hunted by other men. So *Dxui* became the tears of men. Then, as if at last to escape, he flew away

[1] Dietrich Bonhoeffer, op. cit., p. 179, translation by James Mark, from *Prism*, VI, 2 (1962).

to the place of his father and mother. But, at the very
moment of reunion with his father, he turned into a
lizard, clinging close to the dust. 'To say that *Dxui* died
and became a lizard is the Bushman way of stating that
the first Spirit of Creation is finally and irrevocably committed also to life on earth.'[1]

He that should come, the Emmanuel of Africa's long
dream, is, I believe, this God who has been eternally
committed to, and involved in, the closed circle, even to
the limit of self-extinction. His symbol is not the cross
above the orb, but the cross within the circle. His is the
lost Presence that the primal faith of man has always
sensed. In the meeting of the Christian with the man
who clings to that faith it may be that he will show
himself to them both.

[1] Laurens van der Post, op. cit., pp. 153–6.

8

What is Man?

Abusua nhina ye absua na yefwefwe mmeteme so de (Twi)
We look to those of the stalk but all are members of the family

>>>◇<<<

T HE sense of the personal totality of all being, and of a humanity which embraces the living, the dead and the divinities, fills the background of the primal world-view. But the foreground in which this solidarity becomes sharply defined and directly experienced is the life of the extended family, the clan and the tribe. This is the context in which an African learns to say, I am because I participate. To him the individual is always an abstraction; Man is a family.

It is important to remember what a very new phenomenon, what a monstrosity of human history, one might say, is our isolated man with his intensely private world. J. C. Carothers writes:

Modern Western culture, with its insistence on an individual self-sufficiency which implies the constant need for personal choice and personal decision – the application of general principles to particular situations – is quite a recent thing and dates only from the Protestant and the later Industrial Revolutions. It is far more strange in human history than are the African cultural modes, and carries many risks.[1]

[1] J. C. Carothers, *The African Mind in Health and Disease*, pp. 151–2.

93

The primal understanding of what Man is can be seen sociologically expressed in the traditional pattern of village life throughout Africa. The pattern is being irretrievably smashed. But the idea which it embodied is so central to all primal religion that we must first see what that pattern has been before we can understand the idea itself or discover whether it can survive in new forms.

One such village which I have known in Northern Rhodesia may serve as an example – it has been fully described by Dr Dorothea Lehmann in *Christians of the Copperbelt*, chapters 4 and 5. The heart of the village consisted of the home of the present headman, surrounded by eleven other houses in which lived four generations of those who were most closely related to him by the maternal line of descent – his mother, and her brother's widows and daughter, his own daughters and their families, his unmarried sons, and his sister's family. Beyond this central group lay more than fifty other homes, yet only on the outer fringe were there any inhabitants who were not in some way related to the headman. The very position of each homestead was a physical symbol of relationship, pointing either to the living headman or to his predecessors, so that they, though dead, were continually in the picture. Indeed, had this particular village not been predominantly Christian those forebears would themselves have been represented in symbolic homesteads of their own. The village was essentially the family. It had no place name, but was called by the title of the headman, which he and his predecessors had inherited through many generations from the founder of the family.

What is Man?

Growing up in such a home a small child enjoys a profound sense both of security and obligation. However far it wanders in its play it will probably be within sight of a 'parental' eye to see that it comes to no harm and within reach of a 'parental' arm to administer punishment if required. The girl Nantume in her Buganda village had ten fathers, since every male of that kinship who belonged to the generation preceding her own was called her 'father', and her feeling towards several of them was genuinely filial. Her own begetter might be a feckless drunkard, but there were other fathers to take responsibility for her education and her marriage, and under the protection of the family she enjoyed a measure of safety.

The price of this communal security is an unconditional readiness to share, and a complete surrender of individualism. Often a tiny child may be presented with some tit-bit of food only to have it snatched away and given to an older person in order to teach this lesson. In Nyasaland, when a boy asks an adult for a gift, he says 'Give to me also', unconsciously assuming that he cannot be the sole recipient. A man reared in such a society comes to fear, and to be feared for, any individual idiosyncrasy. Dr Gelfand explains:

he believes that achievement, gain, riches and disparity bring unhappiness in their train. Indeed he may run the risk of being labelled a witch if he gathers around him many worldly goods. Everyone should be the same. Even the newborn babe should be as others.[1]

[1] Michael Gelfand, *Shona Ritual*, p. 4.

95

The nucleus of the family is the father and the child, especially in the patrilineal societies, and the whole pattern of submission and security within the solidarity of the communal bond is an extension of the interplay of parental responsibility and filial piety. First, the son is made to feel his dependence on his parents by virtue of his very birth. This is a recurrent theme in the initiation schools of many Bantu tribes with their symbolic 'visual aids': 'This tough herb, *ikeri*, represents your mother's endurance when giving birth to you: never despise her.' 'This space signifies the yard of your father's house where you kneel to him because he opened for you the door into the world.' Secondly his dependence is brought home to him throughout the long period when he must look to his father for food, protection and instruction. As Dr Audrey Richards has said, 'It is difficult in fact to imagine the extent to which the young boy or man is bound to rely on his father, or the family group, for support.'[1] Finally a youth was traditionally made to feel most acutely his dependence on his father for the cattle of the bridewealth which would enable him at last to achieve a degree of independence by setting up a household of his own.

Yet even after that he remained religiously dependent on his father as his link with the ancestors and the hero-gods. Among the Tallensi of Dahomey a man is not qualified to offer prayer or sacrifice to a lineage ancestor until his own father has passed on; the same is true of the Dinka, the Lugbara, the Shona and many other tribes.

[1] A. I. Richards, *Hunger and Work in a Savage Tribe*, p. 77.

What is Man?

The head of the family is the spiritual, as he is its biological, link with the generations that have gone before.

There is, however, another relationship which to some extent circumvents the absolute authority of the father and by-passes his link with the ancestors. This is the bond between grandchild and grandparents, which is often tender and affectionate. While mothers and fathers are away cultivating, fishing, trading or wage-earning, the youngster naturally spends much of its early years in the care of its grandparents; and many a boy, fearing his father's punishment, has taken refuge in the grandparents' hut. In some tribes young children are 'given' to a grandfather or grandmother for several years. It is a reciprocal arrangement whereby the child serves as a household-help and the old man or woman acts as tutor, counsellor and protector-in-chief. There is no doubt that in primal religion everywhere the link between the alternate generations is regarded as a mystical one. In many parts of Africa it is the grandmother or grandfather who names the infant. The names of the ancestors are tried out in order, beginning with the recently deceased, until the baby indicates in some recognized manner that the choice is right. The shade of that particular ancestor is certainly regarded as taking on the guardianship of the child, and in many places, both in East and West Africa, the evidence points to a belief that, in an undefined way, the ancestor has been 'restored' in the child.[1] Children in Buganda, especially daughters,

[1] Cp. O. F. Raum, *Chaga Childhood*, pp. 67, 159, 297; B. Gutman, *Das Recht der Dschagga*, Munich 1926, p. 314; Taylor, *The Growth of*

write affectionately to their fathers as 'my dearest child', speaking as though they represented the earlier generations; meat sacrificed by the Nyakyusa to a chief who has recently died is given to his youngest grandsons; and in Rhodesia I have heard an old woman say she was returning from her grandmother's funeral but thankful that her grandfather was still with her – pointing to a small boy at her side. This may suggest only that an agglomerate ancestral soul, *itongo* or *ntoro*, is present in the child. But in West Africa, with its typically greater stress upon individual personality, the Yoruba often consult the oracle to determine which of the ancestors has returned in a new-born baby, and Meyerowitz claims that the Akan have a clear doctrine of reincarnation.[1]

This interplay of dependence and responsibility, of filial duty and authority, is not limited to the bond between child, father and grandfather. Those two central links are reduplicated in a chain that stretches out laterally in long lines of brothers, uncles, aunts and cousins, backwards along the line of the ancestors to the legendary founder himself, and forwards down the lineage of the unborn. In the initiation schools for the Chagga boys a girdle of twisted banana fibre is tied round each novice's waist and the accompanying lesson explains that this symbolizes the string that connects him with the ances-

the Church in Buganda, pp. 143–4; Taylor and Lehmann, *Christians of the Copperbelt*, p. 77; Monica Wilson, *Communal Rituals*, p. 162; D. Kidd, *Savage Childhood*, pp. 12–15; J. Middleton, *Lugbara Religion*, p. 28; J. Jahn, *Muntu*, p. 111; S. F. Nadel, *Nupe Religion*, pp. 23-4.

[1] See E. Meyerowitz, *The Sacred State of the Akan*, p. 86, and J. B. Danquah, *The Akan Doctrine of God*, p. 82.

98

What is Man?

tors and which he is now permitted to extend. Seen in this way, Man is literally a family tree, a single branching organism whose existence is continuous through time, and whose roots, though out of sight below the earth, may spread further and wider than all the visible limbs above. Death, it is true, makes a difference: the dead have no life-force, but their power-force is greater and more mysterious. Yet in this single, continuing entity there is no radical distinction of being between that part of the family which is 'here' and that which is 'there'. A son's life is the prolongation of his father's life, of his grandfather's and of the whole lineage. As his father is responsible for him so are they. As he depends on his father so, through his father, he depends on them, and to them all he owes the same filial piety and submission. But his relationship with them may also contain the same tolerant, affectionate respect which exists between him and his grandfather. Man is a family. This living chain of humanity, in which the tides of world-energy ebb and flow most strongly, stands at the heart of the great totality of being and bears the secret of creativity. 'It is Man who counts', says the Twi proverb, 'I call upon gold, it answers not: I call upon drapery, it answers not: it is Man who counts.'

The fact of individuality may often clash with the demands of this collective humanity, just as conflict often arises between father and son, and the occasions for this are far more numerous in these days. Yet the underlying conviction remains that an individual who is cut off from the communal organism is a nothing; whereas even the

99

most anti-social idiosyncrasies may be redeemed by re-
newing the influence of family solidarity. This is asserted
in the Akan myth that the ancestors may be entreated to
change the black Destiny of a man. As the glow of a coal
depends upon its remaining in the fire, so the vitality,
the psychic security, the very humanity of a man, depends on his integration into the family. In the old days
the years of growing up were concerned mainly with his
being grafted into this community; the most important
rituals of adult life were designed to preserve the cohesion
of the community; the important sins were those that
damaged the relationships of the community; and the
most dreaded calamities were childlessness and the breaking of the clan ties, both of which eventually rooted a
man out of the community.

The child is not incorporated into this human organism
merely by birth, just as a Jew does not enter the Covenant
by birth. He is made a member by a series of mystically
creative acts, each like a doorway leading into the next
of a succession of rooms. Step by step the child is made a
member of Mankind. So, for example, in the Meru tribe
to the east of Mount Kenya when a young man has come
through the final stage of his initiation he is given the
title '*Muntu*', man (shortened to M.), which must be
used, like the English 'Mr', before his name for the rest
of his life. The occasion and form of these ceremonies
differ from tribe to tribe, but the traditions of the Chagga
will serve as an example. On the fourth day after birth
the baby was formally presented to the mother's relatives;
and a week later it was accepted with a richer ceremonial

100

What is Man?

into the father's clan. After a month it was taken outside and lifted towards the snowy summit of Kilimanjaro (tribes further south present their infants to the moon) with the prayer, 'God and Guide, lead this child, guard it and let it grow up and arise like smoke!' This might be done several times during the early months. Throughout this time the infant was known as 'an incomplete thing', and in other tribes also a word is used that does not belong to the personal class. The baby was made into a human, after the first tooth appeared, through the ceremony by which an ancestor's name was conferred upon it. Some years later an important step towards manhood was taken with the piercing of the child's ears; this rite created a special link with the paternal grandfather on the one hand and the maternal uncle on the other. The next stage was reached with a ceremony introducing a girl to domestic, and a boy to agricultural, work; as a recognition of their new responsibility the children were allowed for the first time to taste game or beer. From this time onwards the child was made proudly aware of his lineage through the recitation of stories and songs about the founder of his own kinship group. He came to know by heart the names of the ancestors through hearing frequent invocations and myths, and to explain the present by reference back to the beginning of things and to the first man of the tribe from whom that human family had sprung. Then, when about twelve years old, children had the two central teeth of the lower jaw removed by an expert as an offering that linked them directly to this first ancestor. The arrival of puberty was

101

the signal for the greatest transition-rite, namely circumcision, which admitted the boy and girl into full manhood and womanhood within the family. The rising generation from this time was tempted to anticipate its power by throwing off all parental control. The community reacted, therefore, in one last complicated rite, the initiation, which, besides preparing the young men and women for the responsibility of continuing the lineage, impressed upon them that their new-won independence was granted only on condition that they, and the families they were going to found, remained in a filial relationship towards their parents and their ancestors.

Not every tribe has traditionally observed such a careful gradation as this, but all have had some such process of integrating the child into the community. These were the rites of incorporation; all other communal ceremonies were rites of consolidation. Through the former a person was made man by being grafted into the living human organism, namely the family; through the latter full manhood was maintained by restoring the solidarity wherever it might be threatened, either by disruption within or by misfortune from outside. The planting of a new food garden, the building of a new homestead, preparations for a journey, the betrothal of a couple, prolonged childlessness, a case of sickness, serious indiscipline, a death in the family – these were occasions for rallying the whole *family* group[1]: the three or four generations of the living and the immediately anterior generations

[1] T. C. Young, *African Ways and Wisdom*, p. 56.

of the dead who belonged especially to that smaller unit.
The head of the family was the link between the seen
and the unseen members; through his acts and words
communion was renewed, discord was healed, and the
advice and powerful aid of the 'elders' was enlisted.
Matters of wider concern, such as the installation of an
important heir, might call for a representative gathering
of the whole *clan*, with the clan divinities as the true
'elders' of that unit. But a general contingency – the
start of the planting season, the eating of the first fruits,
prolonged drought, pests that destroy the crops, widespread epidemics, invasion, rebellion, succession to the
chieftainship – required a tribal ritual and an appeal to
the hero-gods and founders of the *tribe*.

As an example of *family* ritual, apart from the daily
sprinkling of flour or libation or drink for 'the elders'
which may take place at each homestead, we may cite
an instance recorded by Dr Gelfand in the Mount Darwin
district of Southern Rhodesia.[1] A younger brother of the
head of the family was sick. Guided by the diviner, they
decided to enlist the help of their grandfather's shade.
The sick man's son-in-law gave a bull for the sacrifice
and a nephew of the deceased grandfather, being closest
to the dead by reason of age (though not in direct
succession), dedicated it, throwing some grains of millet
across its back and saying, 'You, uncle, this is your ox.
Keep us well and do not cause illness among us.' Then
all the relatives sitting around clapped their hands as a
sign of their reverence to the dead. Soon afterwards the

[1] Michael Gelfand, *Medicine and Magic of the Mashona*, pp. 50–1.

sick man recovered and a day was fixed on which the bull that they had pledged was to be killed. The head of the family gave his wives millet to brew beer. As many of the family as possible gathered to spend the night before the sacrifice in drinking and singing. In the morning they met beneath a large *mutuwa* tree, sacred to such ceremonies, where a man who had been a close friend of the dead grandfather supervised the digging of two pits and the erection of a fence around them and the tree. The brothers-in-law of the man who was sick covered the bull ceremonially with a black cloth which they had purchased and led it into this enclosure, where the friend of the grandfather cut its throat. The flesh was roasted on a fire outside the fence and then carried back into the enclosure. There the head of the family stood and addressed the grandfather's shade saying, 'I am your grandson. I have given you this meat so that you can stay with us. If you see a witch coming to trouble us drive her away.' Each of the relatives then entered the enclosure in turn and taking a piece of the meat, announced his particular relationship to the grandfather and asked for his blessing. Then he threw the meat into one of the pits. When all had done this the head of the family returned into the enclosure with two of his wives, each bearing a pot of beer. Again he addressed the shade, saying, 'Grandfather, you may think your family has only given you meat. But that is not so. We want you to drink as well, because the meat makes you thirsty.' Then one of the pots of beer was poured into the second pit. The other pot of beer was presented to those relatives and friends who had played a special part in the ceremony. The whole family then bade farewell to the grandfather by clapping their hands and returned to the village with the remainder of the meat. This was carefully apportioned and eaten with beer in their separate homesteads.

The *tribal* ritual is essentially a projection of the family ritual on to a wider screen. Very rarely does it involve an assemblage of large numbers of the tribe. The ceremony is an esoteric one, carried out by representative heads and hereditary priests. Monica Wilson has described[1] an occasion in 1935 when a prolonged spell of hot dry weather, accompanied by locusts, was seriously affecting the food supplies of two related tribes, the Kinga and the Nyakyusa, who looked back to a common ancestry of hero-gods. One of these was *Lwembe* whose home, and subsequent shrine, was at a place called Lubaga. The initiative came from an important chief of the Kinga who, at the injunction of one of their prophets, sent two priests with their young grandsons to Lubaga; there they were joined by five Nyakyusa chiefs of the royal lineage that *Lwembe* founded, four hereditary priests of the Lubaga shrine, and Kasitile, another priest, whom we have already encountered in Chapter 3. There was also a small crowd of Nyakyusa commoners. They entered the sacred grove with a small bull brought by the senior chief of the Nyakyusa and three large gourds, one of milk, one of the bamboo beer of the Kinga and one of Nyakyusa millet beer. These were poured out at the foot of a particular tree while three of the priests addressed *Lwembe*

[1] Monica Wilson, *Communal Rituals of the Nyakyusa*, pp. 30–3.

105

and several of his descendants by name, telling them of
their hunger and of the locusts and begging for rain and
fertility. The bull should have been killed by the senior
chief, but as he was old and ailing, the task was performed
by his younger brother. Meat was cut from the forelegs –
the joint which is reserved by the Nyakyusa for the
shades – and offered to *Lwembe*. The shouting, chattering
crowd had first to be silenced. Then the senior chief and
one of the Kinga priests threw the pieces of meat into a
hollow in the soil, saying 'O thou *Lwembe*, thou *Mwam-
pondele*, stand by us. This is your bull. Give us children,
milk, cattle, food; may sickness be slight. Stand by us.'
Then the two Kinga grandchildren, representing, as we
have seen, the ancestors in their own persons, were given
strips of the cooked meat to eat and some of the bamboo
beer to drink. Finally the bulk of the cooked meat was
divided out for all the participants to take away with
them, though there was some quarrelling between the
two tribes as to what was each party's proper portion.
After this ceremony all who had officiated in any way
held themselves apart from their wives and children for
several days and nights, for, as one of them explained,
'We say, "Let us wash and anoint ourselves and be alone
until that lord has gone out of our bodies, since we were
in the ritual".'

One or two points emerge from these two instances
which deserve note as being generally true of similar
rituals throughout Africa.

Whether they are to be regarded as 'worship' or not,
these ceremonies are what Anglicans would call 'Occa-

What is Man?

sional Offices'. Apart from certain tribal rituals at seed time and harvest, and some isolated observances of the moon's phases, ritual assemblies in Africa do not take place at regular intervals like the Christian or Muslim 'sabbaths', but are called as occasion arises. The annual festivals in West Africa might be regarded as an exception to this, but even they are related to natural contingencies such as the beginning of the rains, and the actual date is determined year by year by the priests or diviners of the cult.

It follows from this that the function of these rites is related to specific needs rather than to any inherent value or necessity in the act of worship itself. The sentiment which inspires them is not a mystical response to the numinous; it is frankly self-regarding and utilitarian. That does not mean it is selfish and materialistic; for the rites are never carried out for an individual's benefit alone, even in the case of the sick man, but for the peace and well-being of the community. On another occasion the Nyakyusa priest, Kasitile, arrived at the shrine at Lubaga because a local prophet in his area had foretold famine and he himself was ailing. To the priest of the sacred grove he explained his business in these words:

The sky has made us still and silent. We long for the grove; since Mwakisisya died we have wished for it. We have come to beg. I lie down wrapped in mats but the cold will not leave me. So I said to myself, 'Let me go to my father, let me go to my mother'. I am hungry. Have I food? The earth is destroyed.[1]

[1] Monica Wilson, *Communal Rituals of the Nyakyusa*, p. 35.

This African prodigal son was concerned less with his personal restoration than with the reconciliation of the whole family. For, as we have seen, these communal rituals are essentially a family conclave. Relatives do not assemble, however, even when some of them are dead merely to contemplate one another or enjoy a mystical communion, but to resolve their differences, to do business, to meet some special need, or to maintain their solidarity by fulfilling their various responsibilities and obligations to one another.

Responsibility and obligation – those are the operative words. The human solidarities of Africa do not depend upon the changes and chances of affection. The family is a delicately poised and interlacing organism in which each knows to whom he owes particular duties, from whom he can expect particular rights, and for whom he bears particular responsibilities. And this whole pattern of interdependence is symbolized and ratified by the way in which food is provided from one household and shared amongst others. The central feature of these rituals, therefore, is not a communion through eating and drinking together but a recognition and acceptance of the pattern of mutual obligation through the division of food according to the rules of kinship. When a bull is sacrificed by the Dinka every joint and cut is allocated according to an unchanged plan – this leg to the brothers of the sacrificer, that to his maternal kin, one part to his eldest sons, another to the youngest, the head to the old people of the village, the hump to the ancestral divinity, and so on. For, as a Dinka chief explained it, 'The people are put

108

together, as a bull is put together.' Godfrey Lienhardt writes:

Since every bull or ox is destined ultimately for sacrifice, each one demonstrates, potentially, the ordered social relationships of the sacrificing group, the members of which are indeed 'put together' in each beast and represented in their precise relations to each other in the meat which it provides.[1]

The sacrifice is above all an affirmation that 'all the members of the body, being many, are one body', and this unity is built of mutual obligation. Dr Richards says of the Southern Bantu:

The ritual meal binds the living and the dead to fulfil their part in this complex scheme of family obligations. It expresses the tie of child to father, father to child and that of the man and his relatives. All share in the general sense of rejoicing and delight in the feast of meat, but each is keenly aware by whom the beasts have been provided, according to what scheme they have been divided and what obligation they lay on a particular ancestral group. . . . Concrete demands are made of the spirits, to which the sacrifice pledges them to accede. . . . All those benefits, in fact, for which the son depended on his father on earth, the spirit is pledged to give to his descendants by the sacrifice he receives.[2]

It is in this setting of the family organism that we have to understand the traditional African concept of marriage. This book cannot include an adequate discussion of the subject, though it is of crucial importance to the encounter of Christianity and primal religion. I would only enter a plea to the Churches in Africa not to isolate the

[1] See Godfrey Lienhardt, *Divinity and Experience*, pp. 23, 24.
[2] A. I. Richards, op. cit., pp. 187, 185.

109

difficult questions concerning marriage from the total African view of what Man is.

After the long gradations of childhood, the wonder of sexual maturity lies in the fact that by its means a boy or girl literally attains Man-hood and becomes a link in the living chain of humanity. This newly quickened power is the most intense expression of the life-force, and the young walk proudly. '*Okyali muto*, You are still a child', you may say jokingly to a young girl. And softly but with immense confidence she may reply, '*Ndi mukulu*', which may mean, 'I am older than that', or 'I have reached maturity', or even 'I am no longer a virgin.' For sex is good, and the joy of it goes far beyond its physical pleasures and outshines even the shame, which may be great, of breaking the bounds. Africa has not always agreed with Europe as to what was right or wrong in this sphere, but traditionally there have always been strict controls and sanctions. The fact that these have so widely broken down under the impact of social change is Europe's problem as much as Africa's today.

The transfer of a girl and all her unborn children from one kinship group to become a wife in another represented a very serious loss of the life-force of her family which must be compensated by some exchange. The classical form of bridewealth was a transfer of cattle which, as we have seen, were symbolic of the family group to which they belonged. The transaction was a public, ceremonial event, for the greater the number of kinsmen who contributed to the gift, or who shared in receiving it, the greater was the security of the marriage. These cattle were rarely sold, at least during the early years of the marriage. Since they had to be returned if the marriage broke down, they were a pledge that both families were concerned to ensure its stability. Once again, modern conditions, especially the use of cash, have undermined, and to a large extent changed the significance of, the transaction; yet its underlying concept was sound.

If sexual maturity is the culmination of the boy's or girl's incorporation into Man, its fulfilment is reached in the birth of children through whom Man's continuing life is perpetuated. Childlessness assumes a tragic significance beyond our Western comprehension. To the lineage, living and dead, it represents the threat, and to the father the fact, of extinction. Christian parents who, being childless, agree together that the man should take a second wife and are consequently disciplined by their Church, are in sore need of understanding. Western Europe, rightly or wrongly, has isolated the act of intercourse as the consummation of marriage which, if withheld, provides grounds for nullity. The primal view, regarding the child as the consummation of marriage, considered it more natural that sterility should annul it. It was hard on the childless wife; but she at least had a secure place, in life and after death, in her own kinship group. It is the modern dissolution of that security which, once again, so grievously complicates the problem today.

It is significant that most of this chapter has been written in the past tense. For the solidarity of the extended family and all that was intimately dependent on it, has suffered more disruption from its contact with the modern world than other aspects of the African world-view that were not so tied to a particular sociological expression. As Dr Gelfand says, the attendance of younger men at the communal rituals is very small. Urbanization and a cash economy have smashed the intricate balance of dependence and obligation within the family, and Western education has undermined its sanctions. In the face of this destruction of its outward forms can the primal concept of Man survive?

At least it is not dying easily. Men who have worked for years as isolated, self-sufficient individuals in the mines and factories of South Africa are suddenly seized with an irresistible compulsion to return and sink themselves again in the solidarities of their village home. In that home during all the intervening years they were being remembered and named before the ancestors at every ritual, their absence excused and their protection begged – or similarly included in the intercessions of the local Christian congregation. In the big cities of West Africa scores of separate 'home-town' societies provide the foci of cohesion and loyalty in the population, while workers on the Copperbelt are often caught in a dilemma between the conflicting claims of tribal organization on the one hand and the modern collectives of the unions and political parties on the other. The readiness of coloni-ally defined territories to break up into tribal groups when independence is imminent is another indication that the search for the lost solidarities has not been abandoned.

The Church in Africa is turning its attention to the areas where the breakdown of those solidarities is most

evident. Those are the great areas of 'need'; and the
Gospel meets them by rescuing the rootless individual
and trying to integrate him into a modern society; by dis-
ciplining and forgiving those whose married life has gone
astray and training them in Western patterns of home-
making; by rehabilitating the delinquent and giving
Christian insights to the new leaders; and by offering the
fellowship of the Church to supersede the security of the
family. Christ is the Divine Servant and areas of need
are the context *par excellence* of his Servanthood.

But areas of need are not, surely, the limit of his
Realm. His is no carrion-comfort feeding on dissolution;
and his presence with Man is not only at the place of his
defeat but also at the place of his vision, to preserve and
fulfil whatever in it has been true and strong. It is the
lordship of Christ which is in question. Either he is the
Lord of all possible worlds and of all human cultures, or
he is Lord of one world and one culture only. Either we
must think of the Christian Mission in terms of bringing
the Muslim, the Hindu, the Animist into Christendom,
or we must go with Christ as he stands in the midst of
Islam, of Hinduism, of the primal world-view, and watch
with him, fearfully and wonderingly, as he becomes –
dare we say it? – Muslim or Hindu or Animist, as once
he became Man, and a Jew. Once, led by the Spirit, the
Church made its choice in this matter at the Council of
Jerusalem and dared to win the Gentiles by becoming
Gentile. Paul and those who followed him did not wait
for history to reduce the Graeco-Roman world to chaos
and drive its derelicts into the arms of the Church. They

claimed that world in its strength and reformulated the Gospel in the terms of its wisdom. So Christ in his Church answered the call of the Greeks; he came where they were and became what they were. From within their own culture he challenged their strength and judged their wisdom. He turned their world upside down, just as he had turned Judaism upside down – just as, indeed, if he enters our Churches today, he turns our Christianity upside down. So would he challenge and judge and revolutionize the African world-view; but he must do it from the inside.

The Church, unfortunately, has too often retreated from the bold position of the Council of Jerusalem and demanded of its converts some cultural equivalent of circumcision. It is sufficient to mention three such demands – monogamy, teetotalism, and actually, in some areas, uncircumcision – for most of us to rally, as modern Judaizers, in defence of the Law. We expect the peasant to opt out of the ancient solidarities of family and tribe and become individualized so as to make those personal choices and separations of himself from the mass which we find central to the Christian experience. And, if he is not ready to capitulate, we wait for the forces of change and disruption to break down his defences. They are doing so with grim efficiency, but can we be so confident that they are God's allies?

A missionary who has worked among the Magazawa in Northern Nigeria does not think so. He writes:

Pagan parents have repeatedly said to me, 'Do not take our children from us ' The neighbouring Muslims, who delight to

114

What is Man?

speak in proverbs, have told them that Europeans eat people. It is a reference, I believe, to the change we make in children and grown-ups when we have converted them to the Western interpretation of Christianity. We are the modern cannibals who eat a man's personality and leave him an unattractive, rude specimen of humanity, out of harmony with himself and those with whom he has to live. What the Muslim neighbours are saying is: 'We and you have a religion which synchronizes with the rhythm of our community. Refuse to surrender it for an unharmonious city religion lived in an atmosphere of extreme individual loneliness.'

In a time of cultural disruption the best in the vanishing society are often those who will not abandon the old values and the old solidarities to win a private salvation. Kasitile the priest was one of these. He said to Godfrey Wilson:

If it were not for the ritual I would get you to speak to the Europeans of the Mission, and I would go with my wife, Jane, and be baptized. If my son was old enough and had agreed to carry on the ritual I would do it; perhaps I will when I am old . . . it is good to have one's heart washed clean, we are dirty inside. The Christians say to us: 'You, with your four wives each, you are all dirty, you love one and squabble with the rest.' Well, it is so with me, I love Jane only; I would like to go and be baptized with her. But I fear for the ritual, I fear hunger, the hunger of the people. For I am the food of the country, I am the maker of food.[1]

Kasitile's dilemma is essentially the one which I found myself facing at the end of my study of the Church in Buganda. I hope I may without presumption quote the paragraph which closed that book, for it is the point from

[1] Monica Wilson, op. cit., p. 141.

115

which I am now compelled to go forward in the attempt to answer the question which then confronted me.

The question is, rather, whether in Buganda, and elsewhere in Africa, the Church will be enabled by God's grace to discover a new synthesis between a saving Gospel and a total, unbroken unity of society. For there are many who feel that the spiritual sickness of the West, which reveals itself in the divorce of the sacred from the secular, of the cerebral from the instinctive, and in the loneliness and homelessness of individualism, may be healed through a recovery of the wisdom which Africa has not yet thrown away. The world Church awaits something new out of Africa. The church in Buganda, and in many other parts of the continent, by obedient response to God's calling, for all its sinfulness and bewilderment, may yet become the agent through whom the Holy Spirit will teach his people everywhere how to be in Christ without ceasing to be involved in mankind.[1]

[1] John V. Taylor, *The Growth of the Church in Buganda*, p. 259.

116

9

The Second Adam

Ndagizwa si urindzi, urindzi ni mwenye (Nyika)
Guardianship is not to give an order but to give one's self

F or a Christian from Europe or America the meeting
with those who hold this primal view of Man ought to be
a profoundly humbling and disturbing experience. He
knows already, if he is in touch with the movements of
theology, that the Christian understanding of Man has
far more in common with the solidarities of Africa than
with the individualism of the Western World. But it is
one thing for him to know this as a piece of biblical
doctrine, and quite another to be compelled to struggle
out of the thought-patterns of his own culture and learn
from Africa how to see Man as the Bible does.

Taking the Bible as a whole we can find no conception
of man as an individual existing in and for himself, nor
is its attention focused upon the individual's relation to
God. The Christian can never truly say 'I am man', but
only 'I am in Man'; he exists not in his identity but in
his involvement. We are members one of another by
virtue of the biological links of family and race, by virtue
of our interdependence in society and culture, by virtue
of the history and nationality that bind us to a particular
past and future. The Bible takes all these factors seriously,

117

never dismissing them as incidental or irrelevant, because they are all strands of that web of relationship that makes us one and binds us 'in the bundle of the living with the Lord our God'.

The Bible recognizes also the ultimate dread and dereliction of isolation. This was the curse laid upon Cain, to be cut off from man's natural relationship with the soil and with society, and it was more than he could bear.[1] The punishment for the most heinous offences was that the individual, family or tribe should be 'cut off from among the people'.[2] Conversely the blessings that are promised to those who maintain a right relationship with God are always communal, a share in the *shalom*, the peace of the People of God.[3]

For human destiny, according to the Bible, is the destiny of a 'people'. The word (Hebrew '*am*, Greek *laos*) is central and it bears very close affinities to the Africans' understanding of Man, with their continual reference back to the beginning to an original ancestor from whom the branching organism of their human stock had sprung, and to the great names of the lineage that followed after. Dr Sundkler has most movingly described how 'the Old Testament in the African setting is not just a book of reference. It becomes a source of *remembrance*. The African preacher feels that Genesis belongs to him and his Church, or rather vice versa – that he and his African Church belong to those things which were in the begin-

[1] Gen. 4.11–14.
[2] Gen. 17.14; Exod. 12.17; Lev. 18.29, etc.; Ezek. 14.8; I Kings 9.7, 14.14; cp. Ruth 4.10.
[3] Gen. 12.2, 3; Deut. 28.8, 9; Ps. 29.11; Gal. 6.16.

118

The Second Adam

ning.'[1] Every African understands the inner imperative to 'look to the rock whence ye were hewn, look unto Abraham your father'; and time would never fail him to tell of Gideon, Barak, Samson, Jephthah, of David and Samuel and the prophets. Professor Ernest Wright says:

The conception of 'the children of Israel' as a term for the people involved a psychic unity and was traditionally simplified after the patriarchal pattern by the assumption of a common ancestor. . . . Even in the Gentile Church continuity with the old ideal was preserved in the teaching that Christians are children of Abraham by faith and adoption . . . to belong to the community is to share the life of a 'people', and the conception of 'people' arose from the understanding of kinship, starting in the father's household, extending to the family, and finally to all kinsmen who take part in the whole of the common history.[2]

It is true, as Professor Wright goes on to point out, that the factors of race, blood and genealogy would never in themselves have created Israel. But the African knows this also from his own experience and understanding of clan and tribe. He is made a member – made, indeed, a man – not by birth but by the rites of incorporation, some of which may actually have symbolized a death and rebirth for him. His continuing membership depends on the other rites which maintain him in the bonds of community, and on the laws and customs which ensure its well-being. In his case, as in the Jew's, significance and ultimate survival are the boons of a covenant of mutual responsibility and obligation.

[1] Bengt Sundkler, *The Christian Ministry in Africa*, pp. 282–7.
[2] G. Ernest Wright, *The Biblical Doctrine of Man in Society*, SCM Press 1954, pp. 49, 51.

Thus far the Christian African, if he is not misled, will give glad assent to all the insights of his own culture, and the Christian from the West, if he has understood, will sit as pupil to the 'pagan' to re-learn the primal vision. But at this point in their conversation, if it has been humble and open, Christ confronts both the 'pagan' and the Christian with crisis. The 'pagan' sees the *Erchomenos,* the Coming One, standing in the midst of his own world-view and presenting to him several points of reference so relevant and yet so startlingly new as to command immediate recognition and immediate resistance. The Christian also, looking through African eyes, sees how starkly revolutionary those points of reference are, and is compelled to face elements in his Gospel which he himself has evaded in the practice of his religion. So both are brought to self-judgement and decision.

What are these points of reference which constitute such a new set of criteria? In a word, Jesus simply points men further back and further forward. This widening of the frame to the ultimate Beginning and End is the same utterly simple move by which he confounded the Jewish faith and drove it to crucify him. In his arguments with the Jewish theologians about divorce Jesus cut across their casuistry by setting marriage within the context of the divine beginning – 'In the beginning, at the creation, God made them male and female' – and of the divine end – 'They are sons of God because they share in the resurrection.' Again, by applying the same framework of the ultimate Alpha and Omega, he broke open the bounds of their narrow, nationalist Salvation-history –

The Second Adam

'Before Abraham was, I am,' and, 'They shall come from the east and west and from the north and south and shall sit down in the Kingdom of God.' Exactly the same thing happens when Christ speaks to the traditional thought of Africa.

To the African world-view the first overwhelming surprise of the Gospel comes from the recognition that the solidarity of human life is related directly to God. The covenant of mutual responsibility and obligation is not merely betwixt kinsmen, but between the people and God. Let us grant that in a few areas of Africa this has always been known. Among the Meru of Kenya, for example, the *Mugwe*, from whom every sub-tribe derives its solidarity, can only be the source of blessing to his people inasmuch as he maintains his uniquely close relationship to God. It is to God that he addresses all his prayers on behalf of his people, never to the ancestors. In much of West Africa too the ancestors are thought to be more powerful because they stand nearer to the Creator than the living and can mediate to him the prayers of their descendants. But what the Kriges have said of the Lovedu in the Transvaal, is much more generally true, namely that what is significant to them 'is not the origin but the maintenance of the order of nature . . . there is consequently complete discontinuity between mythological origins, or the forces that operated at the dawn of the world, and present realities, or the forces maintaining the existing order'.[1] God may have been the maker of the first ancestor, but the human

[1] *African Worlds*, ed. Daryll Forde, Oxford 1954, p. 60.

organism has become self-contained and self-sufficient in his absence.

But now in Christ the word is whispered that God is inextricably involved in Man. The whole family of Mankind is his creation and his child, on whom he lays an absolute obligation and for whom he takes an absolute responsibility. Every branch and bud of the human tree, continuous through time, is answerable directly and constantly to God, not as an isolated soul but as a member of the whole, just as every cell on the surface of a plant must respond to the sun. This discovery that the vague and distant Creator is the centre and focus of every moment of all being is so catastrophic that it may overshadow for a time everything else in the Gospel.

The second surprise which Christ brings by pointing further back than men have looked is the discovery of Adam. The first ancestor in most African myths is, strictly speaking, the equivalent of Abraham. Most Africans recognize, of course, like the Banyarwanda, that 'all men have indeed a common nature; they are ultimately the descendants of the same ancestor. But this notion does not seem to be very significant, for Banyarwanda are much more impressed by the difference displayed by the various castes.'[1] Our kinship group looks after itself, living and dead together; the other family, the other tribe, presumably has its own independent solidarity, its own ancestors and hero-gods, but that is not our concern. Responsibility and obligation do not extend to the outsider; he may be a threat and in any case is better left

[1] *African Worlds*, ed. Daryll Forde, p. 185.

122

The Second Adam

alone. As the Twi proverb puts it: The stranger who came says he saw no one in the town, and the people he met also say 'We saw no one come.' So Africans have built, and today are still building, their psychic and political security on the old, narrow claim: We have Abraham to our father. But the figure of Adam, when they have discovered him, grips the African villagers, like a revelation, so that they turn back again and again to spell out with undimmed wonder the opening chapters of the Bible. Here is the charter for a human solidarity which can outlast the breakdown of tribal and kinship ties, for they who know a common ancestor must share a common destiny, and the end, like the beginning, must be God's creation.

These two truths – the God and the Man of the first chapter of Genesis – seem to slip so smoothly into the primal view of the world, and yet they disturb it to its depths. They are likely to be met, therefore, with quick recognition and then be rejected, or at least relegated to the edges of awareness as the old picture of things reasserts itself. If the fatherly presence of God is stressed, and the compassion of Jesus, they are fitted into the category of the hero-gods; if the transcendent greatness is emphasized, God goes back behind the clouds, as irrelevant as he was before.

Besides, these two new concepts of God and Man, though they win a strange assent in the heart, are against all the evidence, unless the Christian himself provides the evidence in the way he lives. In the person who claims to have discovered that at the centre of every moment God is present for Man, one expects to see a quality of ardent awareness, of listening and response; in the person who says that as Adam's child he is kinsman to all Mankind, one looks for the glance of recognition and the hand of brotherhood. It is our failure as Christians to provide this evidence that not only confirms the pagan's unbelief but proves our own. For it means that we also have relegated the truth to the edges of our awareness. St Paul's words are devastatingly relevant: 'As you (men of Africa) in times past refused belief in God, yet have now obtained mercy at the very time when they (of the West) refused to believe; even so have they also now refused belief that by the mercy shown to you they also may now obtain mercy. For God has concluded all in refusal of belief that his mercy might be upon all.'[1] We speak to 'pagans', if we speak at all, from within the solidarity of unbelief, the solidarity of Adam. We and they together live still in the primal myth of the lost Presence, of the *Deus Remotus,* because presence is more than we can bear. Our estranged faces are turned away from God, away from Man, away from the brother, to the self-contained sufficiency of the limited kinship group or to the deeper hell of individual isolation. Christians speak, if they speak at all, as the chief of sinners; and yet they speak of his mercy.

There are many forms under which we may speak of Christ. But when our eyes are aligned with the primal vision it is supremely as the Second Adam that we see him matching perfectly the needs and aspirations of that

[1] Rom. 11.30–2.

The Second Adam

world. This, I believe, is the heart of the Gospel for Africa and it was from Africa that I learnt to tell it this way.

'In Adam all . . .' wrote the Apostle, and Africa understands that better than we. She knows what it means to be *in* the first ancestor, to live in the organism which is growing out of him, to be him, his blood still coursing the living veins, his soul infused in the body, his destiny and disposition working itself out through time. But fundamental to that destiny and disposition is the estrangement, the inability to find or face the all-pervading Presence of God. The terror of the Presence, the 'panic' dread, compels Man to make a god who is remote, to raise a hierarchy of intermediaries that thrust him still further away, and to live in a microcosm, making his family unit all in all. Here is the universal irony of Man's situation, that what seems to be a search for God is in fact a flight. Everyman is in Adam, and Adam is hiding from God.

And so the All-Present himself passed into the closed circle of the human family. Stage by stage he was initiated into it as we are; by birth, by circumcision, by presentation with sacrifice, by instruction, by attendance at the feasts, he was made man – 'made of a woman, made under the law'. He begged for the baptism of repentance, immersing himself into a complete participation in our involvement in one another's sin, and in all the effects of our estrangement from himself. As Karl Barth has said, 'He freely entered upon solidarity with our lost and wretched state. So, and only so, *could* the revelation of God to us, our reconciliation with him, take place in him and through him.'[1] As true part of the body that was in flight from God, yet he faced the other way, standing his ground against the headlong spate, and lived every moment towards the Presence of God and towards the presence of his brother. As Man he carried the suffering of Mankind in his heart, he took on himself responsibility for the sin of the whole race, and offered the sacrifice for the cleansing of the land.

But in doing this he was already acting as the Head of the family of man. For that is what he had become. Willingly incorporated into the old Adam for our sakes, by the perfection of his obedience he won back in all things to what Man was meant to be, *in order to reconstitute the whole organism upon himself as the Second Adam.* As the only real Man he offers to us a participation in his Manhood, that we may become a new tree from a new stem. 'I am the Vine, ye are the branches.' Christ could not make us more completely one with himself than he does by imparting to us his name, his own death and resurrection, his blood to course in our veins, his very Spirit infused in our bodies. And all this not for our sakes, nor his, but for the sake of the world. 'I in them and thou in me, that they may be made perfect in one, that the world may know that thou hast sent me, and hast loved them as thou hast loved me.'

From the human aspect it is the response of faith that unites us with Christ, that faith which is a relationship of personal trust and obedience. It involves decision and

[1] Karl Barth, *Church Dogmatics*, I-2, Edinburgh 1956, p. 166.

choice, a change from the old into the new. It is this inescapable element in Christianity which makes it appear that the individual must separate himself from the old solidarity and leap the great divide into the gathered community of the new creation. But in asserting this we must take care lest we read into the Gospel far more of our Western individualism than is actually inherent in it. For the isolated and unrooted, yes, there must be the choice and the leap, since none can enter community by drifting. But what of the person whose identity is not separable from the total organism? Can one who knows that he and his grandfather and his grandsons are one person, one blood, one spirit, come into Christ without them? If a man realizes, as Bonhoeffer did, 'how our centre is outside of ourselves' in emanations of memory, affection and anger, personality and dream, each an autonomous entity at large in the world, can such a scattered self be made over to Christ in a single act of decision?

By opposing the Church and the world, Western theology has drawn a picture of two separate co-existent realms to which the New Testament lends little support. In its pages darkness and light are contrasted, the far are made nigh, the alienated are reconciled. But the simple opposition of two Kingdoms is never stated, and the word *methistemi*, in the sense of transference out of one realm into another, is used only once (Col. 1.13). The typical New Testament word is *metanoia*, which means turning about. The emphasis is entirely on a change of direction, not on a change of position.

The point about Christ is that he is forever in Mankind and of Mankind. He is its saviour, because he is its new head. The Church is that part of the organism which is orientated to the new head and so has become his body. But there are not two bodies. And the *metanoia*, the miraculous turning, is going on within the original organism of Man, and must go on until the whole universe, all in heaven and on earth, is reconciled to Christ and brought into unity in him.[1] As C. S. Lewis has put it, 'A new Nature is being not merely made but made out of an old one. We live amid all the anomalies, inconveniences, hopes and excitements of a house that is being rebuilt. Something is being pulled down and something going up in its place.'[2]

The Christ of the primal world-view demands decision but not disengagement. And the decision may be communal. Walter Freytag, in a supremely important piece of missionary writing, has told how the Neuendettelsauer Mission in their first approach to the Huon peninsular of New Guinea refused to baptize any individuals until the tribe as such had made its response as an unbroken whole and put itself under the 'new morality'. 'The missionaries had the patience to wait for years until the people themselves in their separate tribes came to a kind of national decision, well considered and discussed at length beforehand . . . the conscience of the community was awakened, and this was at the same time the national conscience.' The 'new morality' was not the whole

---

[1] I Cor. 11.3; Eph. 1.10, 22, 5.23; Col. 1.20, 2.19.
[2] C. S. Lewis, *Miracles*, Bles 1947, p. 185.

The Second Adam

Gospel, nor did the people become Christian at one stroke. The changes were concerned mainly with banishing sorcery and blood feuds and the introduction of communal work and communal discipline. Yet the cultural transformation was described by one of those who experienced it in these words: 'At last we saw God and his power. We were filled with joy. We were never weary of learning . . . there arose a questioning and an awakening . . . and since then we have here in the brightness of the light of God a great work, a good road and secure sleep!' When this total reorientation had taken place there was room for personal commitment to Christ and baptism was administered on that basis; but even so it was usually households rather than individuals that took this step.[1]

There is a great difference between that approach and the one which Dr Busia has said was common in Ghana, where missionaries settled across the stream from a pagan village, and there grew up around them a second, Christian village as one by one people crossed over to join them. It is not surprising that in Ghana the Church is still 'an alien institution'.

This is not to say that there should be no crisis, no death and rebirth, no costly holiness. But – and this applies equally where the advent of Christianity has been individualistic – the processes of conversion will be mainly undramatic, and hidden within the fabric of the community. Change should be like a ferment working through the social organism. On closer examination it

[1] Walter Freytag, *Spiritual Revolution in the East*, Lutterworth 1940, pp. 23–30.

will be seen to consist of a multitude of tiny responses,
imperceptible choices, moral and spiritual battles concerning innumerable issues. The accumulated costliness
and pain of such decisions is, I believe, infinitely precious
in the eyes of Christ though there is no crossing of the
river.

For this is the society, we should remember, in which
a baby is not a member of the human race by virtue of his
birth; he is made man by the community through a long
progression of steps. A marriage does not exist through
the single act of two individuals, but is made by the
whole community over a number of years. So it is natural
that a person does not become a Christian through one
rite or one experience, but is made a member of Christ
through a long series of initiations and decisions within
the Body of Christ. A Church that was true to the insights
of Africa would, I believe, have a greater number of
initiatory acts and marked stages of advance, and would
make far more of them. For the Church is the group of
those in the community who are being made members of
the New Man through their interaction upon one another
in Christ.

For if people are to grow into Christ without ceasing
to be involved in Mankind the Word of the Lord will
come to them largely through one another. The direct,
unmediated Voice calls the unique saints like Abraham
and Joan in every generation, but the community hears
it indirectly through its own members. This is demonstrated in the revival movements of Africa, as it was in
the congregations of the Apostolic age. The pages of the

130

The Second Adam

New Testament ring with this note of mutuality – 'Wash one another's feet . . . confess your sins one to another and pray for one another . . . forbearing one another and forgiving each other . . . teaching and admonishing one another . . . comfort one another and build each other up . . . love one another as I have loved you.'

The community there described is not already perfect nor has it already arrived. But it is manifestly alive and moving and becoming. If there is a falling back into sin it is known to friends, challenged and forgiven; the partially blind have others' eyes to guide them forward; the timid draw on others' courage, the stale are renewed by others' inspiration. The prayer of the faithful few who meet daily at dawn in the thatched church is my worship, though I am too careless to join them. The seduction of my neighbour's daughter after the beer-drink is my sin, though I was not there that night. We have 'the same pain and one power'. Every child here is my child to bring up in the fear and nurture of the Lord. Every brother may be my confessor, striving that I may enter in at the straight gate. Like soldiers scaling a wall, we climb upon one another's shoulders and hoist each other up into the City of God.

But if this is the manner in which Christ is drawing all men unto himself, if this is the process by which all things in the heavens and on earth are being summed up in him, then we dare not draw a line around 'the Church' and cut it off from the whole totality. The Church's relation to the World is one of excruciating tension but not separation. Its only border-line consists of hands stretched out and holding on; so is it the Body of the Crucified. There is still an otherness about it because the estranged faces have not yet turned about towards the Second Adam. There *is* a hell, an outer darkness of ultimate isolation, towards which those who cut themselves off are withdrawing. But the Body of Christ remains within the solidarity of Man *because it will not let Man go*. Its pain and tension is symbolized in the words of the young Batak, who said once to Walter Freytag: 'In my co-operation in the national movement I have learned to understand the story of the temptation of Jesus,' and in the testimony of the young Chinese girl, confronting in the days of the revolution a class of excited pupils, 'We love our nation as Christ loved us; can you say more than that?'[1] So the African Christian, knowing both the judgement and the unbreakable love of the Cross, is compelled to love his family, his ancestors, the whole human organism as Christ loved him. Can we say more than that? This is the sense in which the Church universally and locally, has to be a missionary Church. The New Man is 'the man for others'. When the Church ceases to exist for others it ceases to exist.

Christianity, therefore, endorses and fulfils all the human cohesion of African traditional society, but widens its horizons beyond the family and tribe to embrace all Man in a common kinship. Such universality, however, needs breaking down into the existential community of the local groups if Christians are to be fully committed to their membership one of another. The World Church,

---

[1] Walter Freytag, op. cit., p. 244.

The Second Adam

or a pan-denomination, even a province or national Church, make a splendid conceptual back-cloth; but the drama of redemption must be played out on the fore-stage of the local community group. For that is where men are truly present to one another and involved in each other. The fellowship meetings of the revival movements are an attempt to recover this dimension of Christian experience. And Welbourn sees the independent Churches as primarily an expression of the African Christian's need for a group intimate enough for him to feel at home as in the old solidarity. He writes:

The acceptance of Christianity involved a considerable mental adjustment, a scale of thinking bounded no longer by purely local concerns but by a universal God, interpreted by men of a very much wider culture. But it was localized in terms of a few men living round a missionary, with whom they were in close personal contact. As British Government extends, and the numbers of Christians increase, the chief becomes a civil servant and the Church becomes a large-scale institution in which one priest controls twelve or more churches. Economic pressure drives men to work in towns or on distant plantations. The whole basis of personal identity is lost; and it is only the relatively few men, of unusual capacity for adaptation to living on a larger scale who can recover their identity by integration at a more complex level.

So, examining the independent Churches, he concludes,

the primary picture is one of insistence on the genuine autonomy (within a genuine subordination to wider ideal relations) of independent groups in which the personality of life can be regained.[1]

[1] F. B. Welbourn, *East African Rebels*, pp. 201–5.

133

Such an autonomous identity of the local group derives in great measure from its head. If the primal view of man and community is to be taken up and fulfilled in the Church the centrality of the leader in that view must be taken into account. If the congregation is to grow up into Christ within the fabric of society by its hidden responses and mutual caring it will need a special kind of shepherd. So it is to the African understanding of leadership that we must now turn.

10

Prophets, Priests and Kings

Jivuli la mvumo humfinika aliye mbali (Swahili)
*The long shadow of the borassus palm shelters him that
is afar off*

>>>◆<<<

A. *The Mediator*

THERE are many leader-figures in the African scene —
kings, chiefs, elders and headmen, priests, diviners and
oracles, rain-makers, doctors and herbalists. But, broadly
speaking, their functions fall into the two categories of
mediator and medium.

We have already seen the status of the village headman. What he is to the village, the clan-master is to the
clan, and the chief or king is to the tribe. His person is
the sum and substance of the whole community. Many
Bantu people speak of a headman as *mwene-muzi*, the
very-self of the village. Bernardi says the *Mugwe* of the
Meru 'represents the solidarity of the whole tribe', and
long ago the explorer Speke was told that 'Uganda is
personified by Mutesa and no one can say he has seen
Uganda until he has been presented to the King'. He is
the living father of the community upon whom all filial
obedience is focused and who bears ultimate responsibility
for feeding them all. The subjects of an Ila chief are
called his *Baana*, or children, while a Zulu says of his

135

chief, 'He is their father, they his children.' In Buganda the traditional reply when a chief calls is *Wampa!*, 'You have given to me.' Not only food but human vigour and fertility flow from him, and the authority of every father over his own home is derived from him. The Dinka say equally of the eldest son in a family, of a master of the fishing spear (clan-master), or of the tribal prototype Aiwel Longar, that *aa leou*, they prevail. This unique position as representative and life-giver is based upon his function as mediator.

In the first place, as the senior among the living, he is the mediator between them and the dead. Among the Lugbara of north-west Uganda each family cluster has its *bba wara*, big man or elder. He is the ritual representative of the lineage and also the family cluster's head. Besides the shrines of his own recent ancestors he has at his homestead the shrines of the founding ancestors of the lineage. He consults oracles and performs or supervises sacrifices. He also is responsible for the allocation of land. But his ritual duties have priority because of his lineal proximity to the dead. 'Because he is big he is near his father who told him the words of the ancestors.'[1]

The same primary function of headship holds good in the far more advanced and sophisticated societies of West Africa. At the appropriate seasons the head of every lineage among the Ashanti offers food and drink to the ancestors upon the blackened stool which is their shrine, begging for protection and fertility. The central rite of a chief's installation is when he is lowered three times upon

[1] J. Middleton, *Lugbara Religion*, pp. 10–13.

136

the stool of the royal lineage. Thereafter his person is sacred, for he has become the link and intermediary between the living and the dead. At the *Adae* and *Odwera* ceremonies it is he who must offer food and drink to the shades of the past rulers of the tribe. The Ashanti also believe that the land they inhabit belongs to the ancestors from whom they hold it in trust. The chief, therefore, as the representative of the ancestors, is the real owner of the land.[1]

Because this link with the ancestors makes him the fountain-head of the people's vitality, a most important function of the leader in the old days was the blessing of the warriors in time of war. Among the Dinka the invocations and magical rites of the master of the fishing spear used to be as essential for success in war as the skill and bravery of the fighting men. If a clan council of the Meru in Kenya had decided on a raid this could not take place until the young initiate-warriors had received the *Mugwe's* blessing, and on their successful return the victors gave him a large portion of the spoils in thanksgiving.

Secondly, the leader is often mediator between man and the cosmos. His physical fitness or ill-health affects the life of nature, and the 'atmospheric changes' of his emotions are projected into the winds and clouds. A headman in Nyasaland, speaking of his status in the community, said, 'As for me my honour consists in this, that I am the guardian of the cow and the heifer. I care for the little goats and the she-goats, that they may survive

[1] K. A. Busia in *African Worlds* (ed. Daryll Forde), pp. 200–5.

their maladies. In this consists my honour and for this I am desired by my people.'[1] One is reminded of Kasitile's 'I am the food of the country.' The founder ancestors of the chief's lineage were believed to create rain by the virtue in their own bodies, though their descendants often augment this power with medicines or magical objects. Kasitile had inherited from his grandfather five perforated stones with which he performed the rain rituals yet people still connected the weather closely with his personal moods.

Mwaipopo the chief had omitted to tell Kasitile formally that their kinsman, Mwaikyambe, had died. Kasitile had come to the funeral in the morning and gone off in a huff saying, 'They did not tell me.' . . . At about 11 a.m. it began to rain, softly at first and then hard. I was in Mwaipopo's house drinking beer. They discussed the rain, hinting that it was caused by Kasitile. . . . At noon when we got up and went out, the rain had lessened and it stopped almost at once. On my way back from the funeral later, I heard one of the young men, a son of Mwaipopo, who was with me, say to the other: Kasitile has forgiven, but only partially, the rain has spoilt the ritual.

Yet Kasitile himself denied that his own mood or will, or even the magical stones, could bring rain unless the ancestral shades endorsed his feelings and his prayer. He said:

When Kyala hears me then it rains too much, my anger has results. . . . We don't do it ourselves, it rains if the shades and Kyala help us. I cannot say that I do things alone without their help, it is they who give me breath and when they help I feel the power, the rain will fall very heavily.[2]

[1] T. Cullen Young, *African Ways and Wisdom*, p. 125.
[2] Monica Wilson, *Communal Rituals of the Nyakyusa*, p. 117.

138

Prophets, Priests and Kings

So also that unique figure, the Great Queen of the Lovedu tribe in the Transvaal, is so bound up with nature that her emotions affect the rain. Only by proving in the first few months after her accession her ability to make rain is she qualified to succeed to the throne. Yet the Kriges say that for the regulation of the cosmic forces she relies not only on her inherent 'divinity' but also upon the royal rain medicines and, in the last resort, on the agreement of the royal ancestral shades.[1]

Among the Dogon of Mali the clan-master, or *Hogon*, is the representative of his people, but he is assisted by a council of seven notables, the spokesmen of the seven age-classes, and is also the head over the seven totem priests. These two separate groups of eight symbolize the eight first ancestors of the tribe, the eight principal grain seeds of human food, and the eight major stars in the sky. The *Hogon*, therefore, contains and controls in his person the unbroken life of mankind, the rhythm of cultivation, and the cosmic rhythm of the universe. Both the design of his house and the colours of his ceremonial garments are also a symbolic microcosm.

If the father of the people is also the personification of the life of nature it is not surprising that the ebbing of his vitality should be regarded as a calamity at all costs to be avoided. So, before life begins to fail, the queen of the Lovedu must take poison, the ruling *Lwembe* of the Nyakyusa is smothered by the commoner priests, and the Dinka master of the fishing spear goes down with dignity, or did, alive into his own grave.

[1] J. D. and E. J. Krige in *African Worlds*, p. 65.

Not all tribal chiefs, of course, are the controllers of nature and the rain-makers. In fertile areas the lack of rain is never an issue, and elsewhere many tribes have professional rain-makers independent of the chiefs. Quite often, however, it will be found, as among the Nyakyusa, that these originally had their powers delegated to them by an earlier generation of chiefs. Dynasties of conquerors, also, do not owe their position to any mystical link with nature. In Dahomey the monarchy was imposed by invasion and the king was essentially a war-lord and popular leader rather than a mythological and ritual figure. In military tribes such as the Zulu or Tsonga the mystical relation of the chief to his people is not based upon his natural fatherhood in the lineage but has to be achieved rather through magical strengthening on his accession, and his power over nature depends largely on the royal regalia which he inherits. Lord Hailey has also contrasted the northern with the southern tribes of Uganda. In the loosely organized northern tribes the chief, as in some Nigerian tribes, is 'one of the people derived of, and related by blood to them', and so 'obliged to consult and act in accordance with the people's wishes'. But in the south this sense of community between chief and people is absent. He is lord rather than father, and so is more free to make innovations in tribal custom and come to terms with alien cultures.[1]

The third mediatorial and priestly relationship of the traditional leader is the link he has with God. This, of course, does not operate among the peoples who believe

[1] A. I. Richards, *East African Chiefs*, p. 347.

Prophets, Priests and Kings

God is too remote for any human access. But the Dinka regard their masters of the fishing spear as representing their first ancestor and hero, Aiwel Longar, whom they speak of as the eldest son of Divinity. Lienhardt says:

As such he shares something more of the 'father's' nature than do other men, and is for that reason a point at which men and Divinity meet. . . . He represents man to the divine; he mediates the divine to men. This mediation of Dinka spear-masters and prophets, made possible by a combination analogous to that in the eldest son of the dual roles of son and father, is one of the most important concomitants, for Dinka social structure, of the attribution of transcendental fatherhood to Divinity.[1]

The *Mugwe* of the Meru clans closely resembles the judges of the Hebrew theocracy or the prophet Samuel, 'a leader rather than a ruler, a prophet rather than a priest'.[2] In his official capacity he prays not to the ancestors but only to God. An example of this intercession is given by Bernardi; it was addressed by the *Mugwe* of the Imenti clan to God, 'the possessor of brightness', whose symbolic abode is the snow-crowned peak of Mount Kenya. In the vernacular it is in rhythmic speech.

Kirinyaga, owner of all things, I pray thee give me what I need, because I am suffering, and my children too, and all the things that are in this country of mine. I beg thee for life, rich life, and healthy people with no disease. May they bear healthy children. And also to women who suffer because they are barren, open the way by which they may see children. Give goats, cattle, food, honey. And, also, the troubles of the other lands that I do not know, remove.

[1] Godfrey Lienhardt, *Divinity and Experience*, pp. 45–6.
[2] B. Bernardi, *The Mugwe*, p. 161.

Another short prayer of his is also recorded, blessing an individual who had come to him for direction and advice. Is it blasphemous to hear in it a faint echo of the seventeenth chapter of St John?

Almighty God, have mercy on me. May this child of mine see these things, so that my work may be seen by all men; and those also who do not trust me, may their infidelity change.[1]

Bernardi's description of the *Mugwe's* office lays special stress on the moral qualities that are required of one who is a mediator with God. He must be 'most pure', 'pure of heart', physically unblemished, a man of noble aims, loyal, of a happy disposition, free from defilement. He should be a well-born person, pure throughout life, not guilty of bloodshed or of anything harmful to his people, faithful to old custom, never intoxicated, able to exercise continency, of irreproachable honesty and kind even to his enemies.[2]

The moral ideal of leadership is almost everywhere the same in Africa and gives a consistent indication of the value judgements of the African world-view. Among the Lugbara 'the ideal of a responsible man's behaviour – and *a fortiori* that of an elder – is that he should be quiet, dignified, slow in decision, just and ready to act in union with his "brother" of the same grade as himself'.[3] The Luhya of Kavirondo think that it is not only seniority which confers rank and authority, but 'wealth, numerous offspring, and a gentle character are looked upon as an

---

[1] B. Bernardi, op. cit., pp. 115–17.   [2] Idem, pp. 105–7.
[3] J. Middleton, op. cit., p. 16.

integral complex' which promotes ritual status.[1] To the Dinka 'a cool mouth and a cool heart . . . are associated with peacefulness, órder, harmony and truth. A man whose tongue and heart are cool is a fit person to adjust the differences between those who quarrel, to see the rights and wrongs of both parties and to reconcile them. This is the character of the ideal master of the fishing spear.'[2]

This ideal which seems compounded partly of Greek stoicism and partly of the later Jewish pattern of wisdom, is well portrayed in Dr Danquah's account of how an *opanyin*, or elected chief, is recognized and acclaimed as such from among the people.

He had married and been given in marriage with honour; he had bought or sold in open or private market with honour; he had been a member of the company of fighting men with honour; he had sowed and reaped with honour; suffered famine or enjoyed plenty with honour; brought up children with honour; worshipped at the shrines with honour; had suffered bereavement with honour; and, above all, had joined with others, or acted by himself, to settle family and other disputes, bringing peace and increase to the family with honour. He had done all these and come up on top without disgrace, without debasement to the dignity of a son of the Akan. This, they say, is surely an *Opanyin*, one fit to rule the family, tribe, clan, or State, anointed head of the people, revelation of God in man, discovered by man.[3]

The final step is the apotheosis of the leader, not merely

[1] Gunter Wagner in *African Worlds*, p. 37.
[2] Godfrey Lienhardt, op. cit., p. 139.
[3] J. B. Danquah, *The Akan Doctrine of God*, p. 122.

to the dread power of a royal ancestor or hero-god, as were the dead kings of Buganda or the Yoruba, but to the level of African 'sainthood', where the human mediator becomes a 'heavenly' guardian and guide. Danquah continues:

And if he passed that further test of patriarch, dying in harness, the *energia* of honour and dignity in him still at a high level without disgrace, then he is truly deifiable, a proved divinity, bearer of the supreme moral ideal, a *Nana*, the exemplar and paradigm of *Nyankopon* (God), what God in himself is, or ought to be.

B. *The Medium*

There is another kind of leader in African society whose function can best be described as revelation. Sometimes the father-head is also the medium through whom the paths of men are lighted. A Dinka said to Godfrey Lienhardt:

See our masters of the fishing spear are like that lamp. Look now it gives a bright light, and we see each other and we see what is here on the table. If the lamp goes dim, we shall not see each other so well, and we shall not see what is on the table. . . . Divinity made our masters of the fishing spear thus to be the lamps of the Dinka.[1]

But even so the Dinka, like Africans everywhere, rely upon special practitioners to bring them a 'supernatural' understanding of events and guidance for action. This is not the place for a full treatment of this fascinating subject. It must suffice to describe three methods of divination and draw a few conclusions.

[1] Godfrey Lienhardt, op. cit., pp. 140–1.

144

Prophets, Priests and Kings

'Throwing the bones' has become a Western stereotype of African mumbo-jumbo, like the 'witchdoctor' and the 'leopard men'. The 'bones' in fact are more often short bars of wood, called *hakata* by the southern Bantu. A set consists of four *hakata*, each with a distinct marking along one side only, called respectively *Chirume,* the male; *Nokwara,* the girl; *Chitokwadzima,* the crocodile; *Kwami,* the mother. When tossed up and allowed to fall, either the blank side of each *hakata* or the carving turns up. There are sixteen possible combinations of carvings and blanks, each of which has a name and a different significance, and the interpretation of these varies according to the matter under investigation – sickness, or litigation, or lost property, or distant relatives, and so on. Though the oracle would appear to be involuntarily determined by the fall of the *hakata,* there is, in fact, some room for human insight in the interpretation. In other areas half-seeds like almond shells are used, six seeds giving seven combinations of convex or concave sides uppermost; elsewhere stones, or an assortment of smaller bones of wild animals are used; but always the principle of chance is the same.

In Nigeria the renowned Ifa system of divination also combines chance and insight, but gives far more scope to the latter. The priest knows by heart a great number of traditional poems, or *odu.* Sitting before a board spread with a thin layer of cassava flour, he tosses up sixteen palm nuts and tries to catch as many as he can. According as he holds an even or odd number, he marks one or two short strokes in the flour. When he has done this eight times he examines the pattern that has resulted, one of 256 possible combinations. This corresponds to one of the *odu*, and from that poem he selects a verse which seems to fit his client's case, recites it and gives the interpretation.

In both the foregoing types of divination what we suppose to be chance is not so regarded, but is sincerely believed to be overruled by the ancestral shades or the hero-god to whom prayer for guidance has been first offered. But the mediumistic aspect of all divination is most dramatically demonstrated when the practitioner becomes possessed; and yet the oracular trance is the method which gives the fullest scope to the diagnostic powers of the human agent. There are some tribes which know possession only as an attack to be cured, like a sickness, by propitiating and driving out the appropriate ancestral shade. But the majority of peoples in all parts of Africa believe also that certain men and women are possessed in order that they may be mediums. Care is taken to discover which of the ancestors or hero-gods wishes to 'ride' or 'be shoulder-borne' on this person, and he or she is then initiated as a professional diviner. The trance is normally induced, usually by prolonged singing, drumming, dancing or the interminable shaking of seeds in a dry gourd, and much more rarely with drugs. Sometimes the medium is assisted by an 'interpreter of the tongues', but in most areas the oracle is directly intelligible.

In the terminology of Western psychiatry the possessed person is in a condition of dissociated personality. Dr

146

Prophets, Priests and Kings

Margaret Field describes it as the 'power of shuttering off the distracting irrelevancies of normal consciousness to concentrate more intensely on a narrowed field', so narrowed indeed that sometimes when the trance has passed little or nothing of it is retained in the memory. This, she says, may heighten 'the ability to concentrate upon a circumscribed set of relevant facts, marshal them and draw conclusions from them more swiftly and ably than the mind beset with the distractions of normal consciousness'.[1] The dissociated mind also has access to recesses of memory that are normally submerged and to the same area of foreknowledge as J. W. Dunne has shown to be thrown open to the dreaming mind. But most commonly it is the collective unconscious and the stereotyped race-memories which well up into the awareness of the diviner and are given expression. To say that the ancestors are speaking is to say the same thing in the terms of a different myth.

The priest-diviners of Ghana, says Dr Field, 'are, for the most part honest men. The phenomenon of dissociated personality, on which their claim to veneration is based, is genuine and impressive. The priests themselves reverence it and submit to severe discipline in its service, though not disdaining its material fruits.'[2] Dr Michael Gelfand pays a similar tribute to the *nganga* of the southern Bantu who combine divination with herbal medicine.

They are keen judges of human behaviour and at the same time botanists of high calibre. Further they believe in their

[1] M. J. Field, *Search for Security*, pp. 55–7.   [2] Idem, p. 74.

147

methods just as doctors in England before the sixteenth century believed in Galen's theories of disease. Their general honesty of purpose and desire to help others possibly accounts to some extent for the great attachment of the population to them. Not that dishonest doctors do not exist amongst them, as the African well realizes. But as a general rule the aim of the *nganga* is to help others and restore them to health.[1]

When his client has left him the diviner of the Luhya sings this prayer song:

Wele, *God, may you help me in my divination*
Together with Muxove *and the ancestral spirits.*
May this man go home and everything turn out right.
It is this which is my food.[2]

In the village where I lived in Buganda was an old woman who practised as a diviner. For much of her time she sat in her doorway watching the world go by; even after dusk she would still be there, recognizing from their footsteps or their murmured words who passed up and down the path. After three months among them I went to her for a consultation; my trouble, genuinely, was insomnia. She took me into the small round hut which was her shrine, with one of my friends and her son. She put the magical *lutembe* necklace over one shoulder, squatted on a reed mat – a Muganda would have used a skin – and began shaking the *nsaasi* gourd rattle in a circular motion at her side. Round and round it swung, the seeds rasping on the dry skin of the gourd, one heavy and three light beats, slow at first then gaining speed like

[1] M. Gelfand, *Medicine and Magic of the Mashona*, p. 97.
[2] Reported by Gunter Wagner in *African Worlds*, p. 46.

148

a train moving off beneath the arched roof of a station; the sibilation dinned on the narrow walls of the hut, on the walls of the brain, till all walls were blurred. She started droning her call to the shades. 'The European has come here. He wants to know what prevents him from sleeping. Come and speak to him. Do not fear.'

After five minutes her body began to shake slightly, and she broke into little whimpering songs to welcome the shades as she felt them approaching. They began to answer with gruff, grunting sounds suppressed deep in her gullet, to which she replied in the same singsong voice, the unrelieved hiss of the rattle dominating all. After a while the intruding voices spoke intelligibly, though still interspersing their open speech with the smothered inward mumbling. *Walukungu*, 'the lion', was the first whose words were recognizable, speaking Luganda, while she as his servant answered him. 'Is this not a bad man?'. 'No he is a good man. He is one with us.' 'What brought him?' 'He cannot sleep. What is it stops him sleeping with real sleep?' 'It is that he refuses to bring the elders to completion, *okumaliriza abakulu*, to discharge fully what the seniors require. It is his grandfather, his father and mother.'

After much repetition the rattle suddenly ceased. The silence startled, like a jerking awake from a dream. She asked if I had understood. Were my grandfather and my parents dead? My grandparents, yes, but my father and mother were alive. She looked into my face a moment as if she thought I was lying. Then the rattle swung again. *Walukungu* returned and with him the voice of a woman,

149

Nabirye, speaking Lusoga. The same diagnosis was re-iterated, 'Do I lie?', asked *Walukungu*. 'I am searching for the cause. He is due to make sacrifice. Let him go kill a white cock. At night let him kill it, naked on the hill, when the moon is full.'

When the seance was over I paid my shilling and left. I was disappointed that the hocus-pocus had been so trite. A white cock at full moon! And her facts were wrong, though she persisted in them. Yet she was no fool nor, I thought, a charlatan. It was only later, when I began learning to think in myth and symbol, that I understood what she had said. For my father and mother *were* dead. I belonged to a generation whose roots had been attenuated and shrivelled. Living our too private lives in our independent homes, we were the victims of the socio-logical pattern; but this did not absolve our conscience for the severance we had had to make, nor for the lost contact we had been too busy to maintain. Guilt and isolation are reasons enough for sleeplessness. My village neighbours had watched a lonely Westerner and their inarticulate diagnosis of his condition had broken surface through the diviner. And what of the white cock, naked-ness and the full moon? They speak of the whiteness of purification, the nakedness of the newborn child, and the full restoration of that which has died. But for those who live in the myth the meaning of the symbol can only come true as the symbol itself is enacted.

Many other types of leader are essentially mediums in the sense that some power not of themselves comes through. It is not the doctor's expertise as a herbalist or bone-setter which gives healing, but the power of God and of the ancestors working through him. For a great part of his work also consists of spiritual diagnosis, revealing the dividedness that makes patients vulnerable or the undetected malice that works as witchcraft.

Essentially mediumistic also are the men whose words have power in the community. Among the Meru the most important elders, below the *Mugwe*, are the *agambi*, the possessors of the word, who, revealing early the gift of special intelligence, are trained from boyhood to be the counsellors of the clan. Everywhere the training of the young was traditionally entrusted to those who had the power to frame their teaching in songs and incantations. For in Africa the word is always a spell that conjures and creates what it speaks of. It is meant to convince, says Jahn, not through logic but through fascination. Until we have understood that, it is a futile impudence to try to tell the African clergy how to preach! Nor will Africa be satisfied by new liturgies made with antiquarian scissors and paste.

c. *Leadership in the Church*

It is not difficult to see that the kind of Church described in the last chapter – localized, involved in the community, growing by many responses into Christ – needs the kind of leadership described in this. A pastor who is one of the people, derived of, and not imposed upon, them; their head because he is their father; authoritative by virtue of seniority and dignity and purity of life; a priestly mediator whose power to bless flows from

151

continual intercession for his people; a shepherd who
'cares for the little goats and the she-goats that they may
survive their maladies'; their ritual representative who
administers the Sacraments in their midst; their link
with the unseen who lives in a deep awareness of the
communion of saints and whose fatherly care will brood
over them when he in his turn has passed beyond. No
peripatetic supervisor can fulfil this role. He must be a
true Elder of the people, supporting himself, if need be,
as a farmer or craftsman, in order that every local congregation may have such a priest.

There is need also for the man set apart by gifts and
training to be the spiritual director and healer – the
Christian 'medium'. Sometimes he may be one and the
same as the father-head already described. More often he
will be the trained professional, and it is such a professional as this that the theological colleges of Africa should
be training. He must know how to interpret the Bible as
a guide for the decisions of daily life; and he must know
how to interpret man and counsel him with as clear
insight as the traditional diviners. For until Christians
can bring to their own ministers their sicknesses and their
feuds, the sterility of their wives and the rebellions of
their sons, with a sure expectation of enlightenment and
healing, they will continue to look elsewhere for help.

It should not be necessary for the Church to duplicate
the conflict that has been created in local government
between out-moded traditionalists and bright young
Africans as alien as the men who trained them. An effi-
cient administrative hierarchy is necessary, and some

ultimate ecclesiastical head, but these should be only a branch of the Ministry. The African Church, like the African State, must have its local autonomies and its visible and actual heads. Nor is there any reason why leadership should not be both traditional and progressive.

11

The Tender Bridge

Kuzimu kuna Mambo (Swahili)
Among the shades there are mighty matters

>>><<<

'SUFFER me first to go and bury my father', said the would-be disciple to Jesus. Since the actual burial would have taken place on the day of his death we must presume that the father was still living and the words meant, 'Let me stay with my father for his last days on earth; when his death has freed me from family ties I will come and follow.' There was a now-or-never urgency in Christ's reply. An obligation that can be ended by death is not worth setting in the balance against the call to eternal life.

But what if the obligation is not ended by death? Had the man been an African he might have said, 'Suffer me first to go and bring my father with me – and all my fathers, for they are not dead but living.' What then would have been the Lord's reply? It is a question that Africa is bound to ask, but so far she has received rather evasive answers.

'Are the people of my past to be forgotten?' asked an African bishop at a recent conference. 'Must they mean nothing to me now?' His cry is echoed in the complaint of the people of north-west Uganda against those of them who had become Christians. 'These people are not real

154

The Tender Bridge

Lugbara. Have they no ancestors? Do they not respect them? Do they not even respect their fathers while they are alive? What will happen to their children if they do not respect their fathers?'[1]

Those words reveal the crux of the misunderstanding that has bedevilled the meeting between the African world-view and Christian thought on this question. To the one what is at stake is the fifth commandment, Honour thy father and thy mother; but to the other, the first commandment, Thou shalt have no other gods before me. But enough has been said in earlier chapters to show that such a term as 'spirit-worship' in this context is doubly misleading. For, as J. H. Driberg has said, 'No African prays to his dead grandfather any more than he "prays" to his living father. In both cases the words employed are the same.' Moreover, the word 'spirit' suggests to us existence of a different kind from that of men on earth. But the African family is a single, continuing unit, conscious of no radical distinction of being between the living and the dead. By sharing food an intimate relationship is reaffirmed, and in that sharing dead and living are present, not as distinct groups, but as members of a single community. Senghor writes of this lack of distinction:

*I do not know when it happened, I always confuse childhood
    and Eden,*
*And I mix up death and life – who are joined by a tender
    bridge.*[2]

[1] J. Middleton, *Lugbara Religion*, p. 35.
[2] Quoted by Ulli Beier in *Black Orpheus*, No. 5, May 1959, Ibadan.

155

There *are* distinctions, of course. The greatest has already been mentioned, it is summed up in Alexis Kagame's epigram. 'The living man is happier than the departed because he is alive. But the departed are more powerful.' This heightening of their power comes partly from a simple extension to them of the awe and dependence that the younger generation feel towards their seniors among the living. But it is probably enhanced also by the sense of guilt which the successor generation inevitably feels towards those it has displaced in the land of the living. As we shall see in the next chapter, there is a strong undercurrent of conflict between father and son in most African societies. This culminates in the father's death by which the son appears to have usurped his parental and ritual authority. Just as in Chapter 5 it was shown that the power of the fetish derived from the guilt of the debtor, externalized and rebounding back upon him, so here too the awesome and unpredictable power of the ancestors is partly a reflection of the guilt of their successors. Meyer Fortes suggests:

It is as if fathers are exorbitantly compensated by society with spiritual powers for being deprived of material powers for the sake of continuity of the society. It reconciles them to their sons who have ousted them and exonerates the latter of guilt, as can be discerned in the funeral ceremonies.[1]

The shades are supposed to inhabit a vague underworld; often they are localized below the ground of the family homestead, or in the food garden, where their

[1] Meyer Fortes, *Oedipus and Job in West African Religion*, p. 49.

bodies lie buried. The little shrines that are built for them or the grove in which the offerings are made, are not their actual abode so much as the focus for the devotion of the living. Their primary concern, to which their concentrated power-force is directed, is always the preservation of the human family to which they still belong, for it is as true of them as of the living that they are because they participate. Hence their continual anxiety lest the living allow them to slip into oblivion or spoil the solidarity and health of the human group by breach of custom or bad relationships. It is this anxiety which gives rise to their attempts to communicate with the living.

Though communication between the living and the dead is so important and may be the source of deep apprehension, yet the manner of it in Africa is more subtle yet simpler and, in a sense, cleaner than the crude occultism of Western necromancy. Europe, not Africa, has materialized its 'ghosts' and called up its dead in visible form. True, southern Africa has a belief that the homeless, alien shade of an immigrant, a miser, or a sorcerer may appear as a flame hovering above the grave and calling to passers-by. Such an apparition is called *sepoko* or *chipoko*; but the word, and perhaps the idea, has been imported from the Afrikaans 'spook'! The great masquerades of West Africa, in which members of the *Egungun* or other secret society invoke the ancestors in visible form, are an entirely different matter. The mask and the dancer concealed beneath it are known for what they are; the awe and danger derive from the belief that at the height of

157

the dance the masquerader is possessed by the shade of the ancestor he is representing. Generally, however, when a man consults a diviner he does not expect his own ancestors to communicate with him as through a Western medium. The voices that speak are those of particular hero-gods or other 'familiars', who diagnose the relationship that needs to be put right.

The direct approach by the ancestors themselves is usually supposed to be made either through sickness or through dreams. Sickness may be caused by the sins or the curse or the witchcraft of a living agent; but very often it is diagnosed as a visitation from the shade of some close relative who has been neglected or who is drawing attention to a breach of the social ethic. Many cases of possession, also, are regarded as maladies requiring cure; the shade has seized the body of the victim and will only leave him when its desire has been satisfied. It is the work of the diviner then to determine which of the shades is making his power felt in this way, what has offended him, and how he can be appeased. Such visitations are occasions for terror. But the shades may also draw near to give guidance and protection. This they normally do in dreams, meeting directly with the dream-soul of the sleeper. A young African on the Rhodesian copperbelt told me this story as a simple matter of fact.

My eyes became very, very bad. I was in hospital for three months and during that time my wife never visited me. The doctor failed to cure me and then he wanted to do an operation. The pain was then so fierce I agreed with him. But that night my father spoke to me. He was very tall and had a long

beard and he was white, not black. Yet I knew it was my
father. He gave me a long white robe with red cuffs and a red
girdle, such as I had often dreamed about as a child. And he
said to me: 'There is no cure for you in this place, but African
medicines will cure you.' The next morning the doctor came
and wanted to syringe my eyes and do the operation. But I
refused. So I was discharged. . . . After two weeks they tried
African medicines but the pain was terrible. Then I began to
dream. At first I knew nothing, only pain. But then my
father came and said 'My son, Benedict, wake up. Go over to
that side and cut down the tree standing by the road. Then
come home and burn it and look at it as it burns. Burn it also
with a castor oil bean.'

On awaking he obeyed these instructions and slept again
the following night.

The next morning I awoke and found all pain was gone. No
weakness. I could use my eyes as before.[1]

But besides such specific visitations, the unseen presence of the dead may impinge at any moment on the
consciousness of the living. 'When an African takes food
or drink', a Nigerian pastor admitted to me recently, 'he
feels an almost irresistible temptation to spill a little on
the ground before he takes it. For he cannot help remembering.' In Uganda when the leaves of the banana
grove shiver suddenly in the heavy noonday stillness, or
the little whirlwinds spiral the dust of the forecourt, the
peasant farmers say the shades are moving about the
homestead, and are glad. Birago Diop, the poet of Mali,
writes:

[1] The full story is recorded in *Christians of the Copperbelt*, pp. 281–3.

159

Those who are dead are never gone:
they are there in the thickening shadow.
The dead are not under the earth:
they are in the tree that rustles,
they are in the wood that groans,
they are in the water that runs,
they are in the water that sleeps,
they are in the hut, they are in the crowd,
the dead are not dead.

Those who are dead are never gone,
they are in the breast of the woman,
they are in the child who is wailing,
and in the firebrand that flames.
The dead are not under the earth:
they are in the fire that is dying,
they are in the grasses that weep,
they are in the whimpering rocks,
they are in the forest, they are in the house,
the dead are not dead.[1]

This strangely mingled sentiment of awe, anxiety and affection which the living feel towards the ancestors is a true replica of the traditional relationship of children to their father. Yet in both love might predominate. An old Zulu long ago described the ritual in these terms –

Their father whom they knew is the head by whom they begin and end in their prayer, for they know him best and his love for his children; they remember his kindness to them whilst he was living; they compare his treatment of them whilst he was living, support themselves by it, and say, 'He will treat us in the same way now he is dead.'[2]

[1] Quoted by Janheinz Jahn, *Muntu*, p. 108, from *Hostice Noires*, ed. Senghor, Paris 1949, p. 144.

[2] H. Callaway, *The Religious System of the Amazulu*, Routledge and Kegan Paul 1870, p. 144.

The Tender Bridge

For their part the living also treat the shades as they did when they were alive – and this means that respect is often incongruously mixed with all the casualness of a normal family conclave. Any European who has been permitted to attend such ceremonies is astonished to find how chatty and unrehearsed they are. Participants may quarrel among themselves as to the correct ritual, and occasionally a statement made to the shades is a blatant deception, as in Ruanda when water is offered while they are told very loudly that it is milk! But generally the form of address is a series of straightforward requests. Praise-names may be used in these 'prayers', but the tone of worship and pleading supplication which appears in prayer to God is significantly absent.

Let the great ones gather! What have we done to suffer so? We do not say, Let so and so come: we say, all! Here your children are in distress. There is not one able to give a drink of water to another. Wherein have we erred? Here is food: we give to you. Aid us, your children.

Such was the address of a Nyasaland headman during an epidemic. Dr Busia reports these words, spoken to the deceased at the burial ceremony in Ghana:

You are leaving us today; we have performed your funeral. Do not let any of us fall ill. Let us get money to pay the expenses of your funeral. Let the women bear children. Life to all of us. Life to the chief.

From the Dinka comes this petition of an uncle on behalf of a sick youth with whom he had quarrelled in the past. This gives cause for an element of confession.

You of my father, I call upon you because my child is ill and
I do not want words of sickness, I do not want words of fever.
You of my father, if you are called, then you will help me
and join yourself with my words. And I did not speak in the
past that my children should become ill; that quarrel is an
old matter.[1]

In many areas, especially in the towns, the cult of the
ancestors is no longer practised as it used to be. At many
points, owing to the influence of Christianity or Islam,
the idea of God is taking over the old prerogatives of the
shades. Today it is often God himself who is thought to
control the fall of the diviner's *hakata* and even to speak
through such famous oracles as Tolonyane of Bechuana-
land. Yet even where the ritual has died, the necessity
to maintain the communion with the dead unbroken is
deeply felt. Many of the 'emancipated', speaking from
within the culture of the West, say the same.

I dream in the intimate semi-darkness of an afternoon.
I am visited by the fatigues of the day,
The deceased of the year, the souvenirs of the decade,
Like the procession of the dead in the village on the horizon
  of the shallow sea.
It is the same sun bedewed with illusions,
The same sky unnerved by hidden presences,
The same sky feared by those who have a reckoning with
  the dead.
And suddenly my dead draw near to me. . . .[2]

Those words have the ring of truth which cannot be

[1] These three addresses are quoted, respectively, from *African Ideas
of God*, ed. E. W. Smith, p. 44; *African Worlds*, ed. Daryll Forde,
p. 201; Godfrey Lienhardt, *Divinity and Experience*, p. 221.
[2] Leopold Senghor, 'Visit', from *Chants pour Naett*, Paris 1949.

achieved by any writer, however sympathetic, who is not rooted, essentially, in the African world-view. Yet they reveal a change of emphasis and an advance of thought from the traditional experience, and the direction of this change is most significant to any who are concerned with the influence of Christ upon that world-view. One might say that love is beginning to cast out fear. The loving affection was always there, but now it is able to predominate and illumine the relationship. There is still 'a reckoning with the dead' to be feared. The Christian must admit that as part of the reckoning with God. But the areas of unmitigated terror have vanished.

For there certainly are such dark areas in the traditional experience. Quite apart from witchcraft, which must be faced in the next chapter, men live amidst powers of pure malevolence. These are thought to be the spiteful shades of those who died in anger against their kin or were driven to suicide or denied the proper funeral rites. The recently dead are dangerous, the 'smell of life' is on them still so they are not accepted into the underworld, neither have they relinquished their physical ties with the living. Those ties must be carefully broken by the living in some ritual act. The touch of death is washed off, or the home fire is extinguished and rekindled; the Baganda hold their *okwabya olumbe* to 'dismantle' death and build the family structure anew by appointing the heir; the Bemba widow is expected to cohabit for a time with a brother of her dead husband in order to break the bond which holds her husband's shade. Without such release or satisfaction the shade becomes an alien, venge-

163

ful spirit, waiting to haunt and attack all and sundry. In Rwanda, indeed, every shade, except a man's direct forebears, is essentially malevolent.

The Gospel has two words to speak in this realm of terror. Neither of them is the futile assurance of a glib rationalism that 'these things do not exist'! The first word is to recognize that there *are* discarnate forces of evil at large in the world, entities of hate and fear and rapacity, whether of human or demonic origin – the devils, elemental spirits, cosmic powers and authorities of the New Testament,[1] but that Christ the Victor, who on the cross stripped them off from himself, is bringing them to naught. The man who commits himself to Christ and binds unto himself his Name and Power can walk without fear. Here is no place for glibness of another kind. The Bible, like Africa, knows well the hideous strength of the things of darkness. They can still strike home, but they cannot separate from the love of God nor snatch any man from his hand. This is another new surprise; for the God who was so remote from human life belonged to an entirely different realm from that of the malignant shades, and none thought to look to him to restrain their assault.

And the second word of the Gospel is that Christ is not only Victor over the powers of evil, but the Deliverer and Life-giver *in the realm of the shades.* Dr Sundkler quotes from an essay by a Zulu Lutheran student which emphasizes this aspect of redemption as the

[1] The usual translations in the New English Bible of the words *daimonia, stoicheia, archai, exousiai.*

164

very heart of the Good News for the African world-view.

The missionaries came with Christianity but missed the open gate for Christianisation. The message was not applied to the existing forms of worship. They brought good news for mankind, containing forgiveness of sins by Christ alone, who died for all and *went to the dead to show them who He was and came up from the dead to show Himself to the living ones*. As the missionaries preached this Christ, they missed the gate . . . they did not encourage and tell them that the Bible itself says that the deceased are not dead but are living or resting, and that their spirits were living because they belonged to God, from whom they came by the creation of Adam.[1]

Expositors of the New Testament are not agreed as to the significance that can honestly be given to those verses (I Peter 3.19; Eph. 4.8-10, Rom. 10.7) which have been adduced to support the doctrine of Christ's triumphal harrowing of Hades. But even without this interpretation, his descent into Hades followed by the resurrection was enough to create a new condition for the dead because the bondage and dominion of death itself was thereby abolished. This break-through was central to the first preaching on the day of Pentecost, and the Early Church enshrined it in the Creed. One of the first cryptic symbols of the Christ was the figure of Orpheus, who had entered the infernal region and charmed its tyrant, and whose music heralded the golden age.

The resurrection of Jesus Christ offers two immense innovations to African thought – the idea that there is *life* for the dead as well as power; and the idea that their present state is not the end of the story. Communion with

[1] Bengt Sundkler, *The Christian Ministry in Africa*, p. 290.

the shades can now mean fellowship with essentially living persons, with whom we look forward to a more intense life than we can now imagine, to which the resurrection of Jesus has already opened the road. Death has deprived them of no more than sleeping does. And even as they sleep they are alive and aware, for, as Africa might put it, in their dream-soul they already dwell in the heavenly country. Among those Nyakyusa who were becoming Christians Monica Wilson noticed that

the supreme attraction, mentioned again and again as the reason for conversion, is: 'There is life' (*ubumi bulipo*). . . . The contrast is between heaven above and the shadowy world 'beneath' of pagan thought. . . . Constantly in sermons by Nyakyusa preachers there was stress on life, resurrection, and on the rewards and punishments of the future life, and this theme recurs again and again in the dreams of Christians.[1]

When the gaze of the living and the dead is focused on Christ himself they have less compulsive need for one another. But need is not the only basis of relationship; and Christ, as the Second Adam, enhances rather than diminishes the intercourse of the whole community from which he can never be separated. Is it not time for the Church to learn to give the Communion of Saints the centrality which the soul of Africa craves? Neither the inhibited silence of the Protestants nor the too-presumptuous schema of Rome allows African Christians to live *with* their dead in the way which they feel profoundly to be true to Man's nature. Said a Roman Catholic of the Lugbara:

[1] Monica Wilson, *Communal Rituals of the Nyakyusa*, p. 187.

166

The Tender Bridge

I do not 'cut' (divide the sacrifice) at the shrine of my lineage, but when my people 'cut' I sit near, since it is my work to 'cut' meat. Some say these things are of Satan, but that is not true. They are good, the things of the ancestors.[1]

Not all are so sure. Others have a more painful sense of conflict such as the African preacher who related this vivid dream to Dr Sundkler.

I saw a mass of people divided into two groups, and they struggled about me. The one group consisted of the old ones from long ago in my clan, and the others were strangers, clad in very shining white clothes and they had crosses in their hands. One group took one of my hands, and the other group the other and they pulled as at tug-of-war. But the strangers won and brought me with them, and they sang a joyful victory song.[2]

But another lay-preacher of the African Methodist Episcopal Church on the Copperbelt found his ancestors echoing God's call to him to be a preacher. While he was sick in hospital he dreamed, as so many do, of the heavenly village across the river. But the angel who stood by him on the bank would not let him swim over, but ordered him to return to his people in the world.

I said, 'Nkosi (Lord)! I don't want to go back to that work where there is too much suffering, and people fighting each other and paying taxes.'
But the man said, 'You must go back in deep believing. . . .'
So I fell back and went on falling down until I returned into that room in the hospital. There I saw my own body lying in the bed. All round there were people wearing long robes. I knew that they were various ancestors although I did

[1] J. Middleton, op. cit., p. 35.
[2] Bengt Sundkler, op. cit., p. 29.

not recognize them. One of them I did know: she was my grandmother who bore my mother. They said to me, 'You must go back now and sleep in that body.'

I said, 'No, I don't want to go back. I want to remain in this body of spirit and I want to go and live in that village over the river.'

But they said, 'No you must go back and preach and believe; and then sometime you will go over the river to that kraal.'[1]

Surely the 'tender bridge' that joins the living and the dead in Christ is prayer. Mutual intercession is the life-blood of the fellowship and what is there in a Christian's death that can possibly check its flow? To ask for the prayers of others in this life, and to know that they rely on mine, does not show any lack of faith in the all-sufficiency of God. Then, in the same faith, let me ask for their prayers still, and offer mine for them, even when death has divided us. They pray for me, I may believe, with clearer understanding, but I for them in ignorance, though still with love. And love, not knowledge, is the substance of prayer.

The content of all such prayer, therefore, should be a form of thanksgiving and the exchange of love and the joy of partnership in God's work and God's praise. None of the classical forms seem to me to be satisfactory. The *requiescant in pace*, in the African as in the mediaeval European setting, hints too strongly at a fear of their restlessness; while prayers of Protestant origin walk so delicately amid their if's and maybe's that they lack the ingenuousness of all sincere prayer. This adaptation of one of them, perhaps, strikes a truer note.

[1] *Christians of the Copperbelt*, pp. 285–6.

The Tender Bridge

O God of the living, in whose embrace all creatures live, in whatever world or condition they may be; we beseech thee for him whose name and dwelling place and every need thou knowest, giving thee thanks for our every remembrance of him. Tell him, O gracious Lord, how much we love him, and grant that this our prayer may minister to his peace; through Jesus Christ our Lord.

If death is what Christians believe it to be, direct address to the dead should be natural and confident. Its essential difference from the traditional address to the shades is that now, since God himself is the Father and Provider concerned in every detail of life, there is no need to ask them for particular benefits which are properly sought from God alone. True to African use it should be wholly distinct from prayer, being rather in the nature of salutation. The blessings and ejaculations of St Paul's epistles, epitomizing the togetherness of the whose fellowship, seem to overleap the narrow stream and to be perfectly fitted for a brief recollection and address to our elders in Christ who have gone before.

Peace be upon you and mercy and upon the whole Israel of God.
The grace of our Lord Jesus Christ be with you. My love be with you all in Christ Jesus. Amen.
The Lord of peace himself give you peace at all times in all ways. The Lord be with you all.
The God of peace himself sanctify you wholly; and may your spirit and soul and body be preserved entire without blame at the coming of our Lord Jesus Christ. Faithful is he that called you who will also do it. Brethren, pray for us.

Such salutations could find a place both in the congre-

169

gation and in the home. For in all our thinking about worship and intercession each needs to remember that no prayer is his alone. The moment I begin to pray I have entered the world of mystical inter-relatedness. My prayer, like a tiny tributary, runs straight into the mainstream of the prayer of all the saints. Something of this mystery was understood by the Dinka who, asking his father's shade for help, cried out,

You of my father, if you are called, then you will help me and join yourself with my words. . . . And you, my prayer, and you prayer of the long distant past, prayer of my ancestors, you are spoken now. Meet together, ee! It is that of my ancestor Guejok, it is not of the tongue only; it is that of Guejok, not of my tongue only.[1]

So our remembrance and commendation of the living dead takes on a special depth of meaning at the Holy Communion where, with all the company of heaven, we know ourselves to be one loaf, one body. Like the blood-stream of that body the quiet flow of mutual love and prayer moves freely between all the members, unhindered by any barrier of space or time or death, and all our caring for each other and all our thankfulness for one another becomes part of the perfect intercession and adoration which Christ our Head is offering, as Man and as Son, to the Father. And, since every meal reflects the significance of that Meal, grace before meat would be in Africa the natural moment for such a salutation to the unseen members of the family. No forms of words could

[1] Godfrey Lienhardt, *Divinity and Experience*, p. 221.

The Tender Bridge

better the ancient greeting: Go with God and let us stay with God.

But must such communion be limited to the Christian dead? That must remain a crucial question for Africa, awaiting the study of her future theologians. We dare not dogmatize in such a realm. Yet I believe the question is very closely linked with the one that was faced in the last chapter – must the Christian be extracted from the solidarity of Man? I ventured to suggest that the relationship of the New Mankind to the Old was one of excruciating tension but not of separation. If that is true at all it must be true of the whole organism, the dead as well as the living. The dream of the tug-of-war was a true picture, but neither hand is meant to let go. The strangers with the crosses in their hands will win in the end but only by pulling all the old ones from long ago into their own realm. The words, 'In Adam all . . .' included the whole family of Man in death; the promise, 'In Christ all . . .' cannot include less than that in life. The genealogies in the Gospel linking Christ himself with the unnumbered myriads of the dead are a symbol of the unbroken cord with which God will finally draw Adam back to Paradise. The Christian's link with his pagan ancestors, in remembrance and unceasing intercession, may be part of that ultimate redemption; for, as Césaire the Martiniquean poet puts it, 'there is room for all of us at the rendezvous of victory'.

12

The Destroyer

Wunyin a, na wunhu; na woye bone de a, wuhu (Twi)
You may not see yourself growing, but you know all right
when you're sinning

>>> ✧ <<<

THE meeting with Christ, in whatever world-view it takes place, invariably brings home to Man how wrong he is. This is part of the very saviourhood of Jesus. Yet so far this book seems to have said little about sin. Perhaps that was to be expected since its subject is the Christian presence among men. For the evangelism that proceeds by listening and learning, entering into another man's vision in order to see Christ in it, does not start with assertions about sin but waits to be told about it. And usually the truth about sin is almost the last truth to be told.

My stay in the Ganda village was almost at an end. I was walking back from a distant hamlet with a man who had spent during the previous months more than three hundred hours as my informant and had become my close friend. We had discussed, I thought, every aspect of Ganda life. As I walked behind him along the narrow path he suddenly said,

'It is not true that we Africans are happier or freer than you are. We all feel your happiness, it is something

172

The Destroyer

we do not know. True, we do not worry as you do; we forget very quickly. But there is no true joy, for we do not treat one another well. We all mistrust one another and there is much jealousy. Africans have no determination. If your work in this place lasted for a year I would give up helping you and grow tired. We do not know how to persevere and endure. Perhaps it is the diet.'

Surprised at this outburst, I asked a few questions and then turned the subject. But a little later he began again.

'We Africans are still children. It is better for us still to be ruled.'

'I don't agree,' I said. 'You are not a child. But in any case, which is the best way to bring up children – the way of law or the way of love?'

'We do not understand loving each other', he answered. 'A man who loves his wife fails to please her and hold her. But if he treats her strictly and with discipline and lays down the law, she understands and respects him and responds.'

'But in your own home', I objected, 'you use the way of love.'

'In my home', he said, 'love is not enough. My wife doesn't understand that I love her. I shall continue to the end. But all think it is foolishness.'

'But what about the children?' I asked. 'They know you love them.'

His face brightened. 'Yes', he said, 'they understand. It is for them we must do it. When they have grown up perhaps the way of love will be enough.'

With his personal problem we had come near to the

heart of the matter, though I was already forewarned not to take his generalized disparagement of Africans too seriously. For I remembered Walter Freytag telling once how he had surprised an ardently nationalist Indian student in the middle of a conversation by asking, 'What is "Indian"?' The answer came quickly: ' "Indian" means idealism, the search for the spiritual realities, renunciation of the material.' The conversation moved on. But more than an hour later the student exclaimed. 'Now I will tell you truly what is "Indian". It is a hopeless inclination to lie. It is limitless cupidity.' 'Both answers', commented Freytag, 'were wrong, of course, but they both gave an insight into the people.'

The sin from which Christ can save Man is not the sin of which others have convicted him, nor the minor failings of his self-idealization nor the exaggerated vices of his self-loathing, but the actual condition of need as he knows it when he faces himself in the presence of Christ, in the context of his own world of thought and experience.

It is often said that, as long as they still share the traditional outlook, Africans have no 'sense of sin'. This is always a superficial judgement but, as far as it goes, it is true of other peoples besides Africans, though for different reasons. In Africa, one reason is the apparent unconcern of both God and the ancestral shades in matters of private and, to a large extent, of public morality. 'Since there is no single sovereign god like Job's, one cannot feel entitled to rewards for following a code of conduct pleasing to him or deserving of punishment for knowingly transgressing it. One lives according to one's mundane

174

lights, guided by the jural and moral sanctions of society, knowing that the ancestors dispense justice by their own standards and that one cannot please all of them at the same time.'[1] 'To the Dinka the moral order is ultimately constituted according to principles which often elude men.'[2] 'In the Rwanda culture . . . *Imana* is not the guardian of the moral order. Sometimes he seems to be regarded as its author in the sense that he might have decided that men should not steal, but it is clear that when a man steals another man's cows, *Imana* is not personally offended.'[3] Obviously, the preaching of the God of Righteousness must create a more vivid conscience as it did among the ancient Hebrews; but its effect is slower than one would expect. When I asked a group of church leaders in the Ganda village what a man can do to please God, one of their seniors replied, 'I have never heard a Christian here ask such a question. People do believe in heaven and hell but most do not care about it. They say, God will forgive me. Their fear is for this life, not the next.'

A second factor is that to some extent the primal world-view belongs to a 'shame-culture' rather than a 'guilt culture'. E. R. Dodds' description of the earliest Greek states might have been written of such people as the Batutsi of Rwanda or the Lugbara.

Homeric man's highest good is not the enjoyment of a quiet conscience but the enjoyment of *timé*, public esteem. . . . And

[1] Meyer Fortes, *Oedipus and Job in West African Religion*, p. 53.
[2] Godfrey Lienhardt, *Divinity and Experience*, p. 54.
[3] *African Worlds*, ed. Daryll Forde, p. 183.

the strongest moral force which Homeric man knows is not the fear of God but respect for public opinion. . . . In such a society anything which exposes a man to the contempt or ridicule of his fellows, which causes him to 'lose face', is felt as unbearable.[1]

Dodds goes on to argue, in a way most relevant to Africa, that the transition to a culture of guilt came about partly because the growing political and economic insecurity, deepening the awareness of human helplessness, gave rise to religious anxiety, and partly because the relaxation of the family bond gave greater occasion for father-son conflict and feelings of guilt in the younger generation. If this is true, then the process must already have gone a long way in Africa.

A third reason for the apparent lack of a 'sense of sin' is that where men feel themselves to exist communally in a personalized world, in which every event raises the question 'Who caused it?', individual responsibility is hard to envisage. Until he has known the searing release of the forgiveness of God, no man can live with his sin; but men have different ways of dealing with it. Because of the different 'myth' of human nature in which each lives, the European represses the things in himself that he is afraid of, the African projects them. The European is on guard against the self he has battened down in his own mind; the African is on guard against the self he has externalized into the world around. Margaret Field tells of a local council clerk who came to a diviner's shrine and 'complained of a sickness sent to him by those from whom

[1] E. R. Dodds, *The Greeks and the Irrational*, pp. 17–18.

176

he had extorted money. He asked for protection from *their* malice but neither expressed contrition nor was given any censure.'[1] In the same vein, Monica Wilson writes:

On one occasion two Christian teachers and a Christian clerk, who had related several stories in which loss of a job was attributed to a curse, asked our opinion of them. When we explained that we thought that the people mentioned had lost their jobs because they were unsatisfactory servants or teachers our friends expressed surprise. 'I had not thought of that' said the clerk.[2]

It is not true, therefore, to assume there is no 'sense of sin' simply because it is not residing in a person's conscience. It may be wandering abroad in disguise — guilt has become a menacing fetish, moral weakness an evil destiny, envy a sorcerer's spell. It needs to be located and brought home.

That can never be done by imposing an extraneous ethic which has not sprung up as the response of the conscience of people themselves. Enough reiteration from the pulpit will successfully establish the new code as the law of the Church; loyalty to the Church, the natural desire to remain in good standing with the group and with God, combined with a fear of divine retribution, will induce acceptance of a kind. But the dichotomy remains between the demands of the Church and the demands of the conscience. The danger in this is not merely that respectability rather than goodness becomes

[1] M. J. Field, *Search for Security*, p. 115.
[2] Monica Wilson, *Communal Rituals of the Nyakyusa*, p. 184.

the aim of Christian living, but that a Christ who releases me from guilt that has been induced, and forgives sins of which the Church but not my conscience has accused me, will not be the Saviour of *my* world. The true Christ of the gospels works more fundamentally. Starting with the question, What wilt thou that I should do unto thee?, he is prepared to be present to the other man with an infinite patience until he himself recognizes and points out the shape of evil in his own world.

The one who is ready to listen rather than to preach soon discovers the conscience that others told him was not there. In spite of the moral unconcern of God and the ancestors in Rwanda culture, for example, 'when a child has disobeyed his father without the latter's knowledge, he thinks not only of the unpleasant consequences that the discovery of his misbehaviour might produce but also (some informants say 'mainly') of the wickedness of the act itself'.[1] Village elders in Northern Rhodesia said, 'An adulterer will feel ashamed in the presence of the woman's husband. even if he is not found out.' 'Two people, both married, who had committed adultery together would feel an equal shame; they would hate each other. afterwards.'[2] The *nkrabea* destiny is to the Akan people the equivalent of the ego-ideal, that image of the self which implies a continual moral imperative.

It is typical, too, of the greater individualism of West Africa that the Akan should teach that after death the

[1] *African Worlds*, p. 183.
[2] John V. Taylor and Dorothea Lehmann, *Christians of the Copperbelt*, p. 299.

The Destroyer

life-soul has to render an account of himself to his late
king who sits in judgement as he did when he ruled on
earth.[1] While from Dahomey comes an unusual traditional song of the divine judgement –

> *Life is like a hill.*
> Mawu *the creator made it steep and slippery,*
> *To right and left deep waters surround it,*
> *You cannot turn back once you start to climb.*
> *You must climb with a load on your head.*
> *A man's arms will not help him, for it's a trial,*
> *The world is a place of trial.*
> *At the gates of the land of the dead*
> *You will pass before a searching Judge,*
> *His justice is true and he will examine your feet,*
> *He will know how to find every stain,*
> *Whether visible or hidden under the skin,*
> *If you have fallen on the way he will know.*
> *If the Judge finds no stains on your feet*
> *Open your belly to joy, for you have overcome*
> *And your belly is clean.*[2]

The moral law, however, is not conceived as an
abstraction which applies equally to all men all the time,
but more as an arbitrary demand which, when it comes,
cannot be disobeyed without sin. On one occasion, when
I had been living on my own in a village for some weeks,
a neighbour who was a professed Christian, offered to
bring a girl to sleep with me. 'I am your friend', he said,
'and I see you like a man in prison. It is too hard.' I
thanked him for his honest concern. 'But I can't do that

[1] E. Meyerowitz, 'The Concept of the Soul among the Akan', in
Africa, XXI (1951), p. 24.
[2] M. Quenum, *Au pays des Fons*, Larose edit. Paris.

to your girl', I said, 'don't you know I am a Christian?'
'You are also a man', was his answer. He argued with
me for a while, then suddenly a new realization seemed
to dawn on him. 'Oh,' he exclaimed, 'if there is *that*
speaking to you, you must never do it. You certainly must
not.' In a most disconcerting way, his attitude was not
far removed from that of the Bible which, according to
Professor Walther Eichrodt, teaches that it is in 'the
unrecurring reality' of particular moments that God's
will 'inexorably calls for a decision here and now and
permits no rest in some secure position which is valid
once for all'.[1]

But the essence of sin in the primal view is that it is
anti-social. The sin that offends God is the sin that is
against Man in his solidarity. The Lugbara distinguish
between 'bad deeds' which are dealt with by human
response such as beating or fighting, and 'sin' which is
mystically punished by God and the ancestors. Sin is
defined as 'destruction' or *'the deed that destroys good
words'*, and refers to any act or attitude of rebellion or
disrespect towards the authority and the established
relationship on which the community is built. To quarrel
with a senior kinsman or to use violence against him, to
commit adultery with a close kinswoman, these are an
attack against the lineage and therefore arouse the wrath
of God. When feuds and offences persist in a particular
family it is seen that God visits it with *nyoka*, his curse,
and it is cut off from the people. 'Because it has forgotten

[1] Walther Eichrodt, *Man in the Old Testament*, SCM Press 1950,
pp. 26–7.

180

The Destroyer

the words of the ancestors it has forgotten the words of God the creator; it is alone and dies out; its words are finished, *nyoka* is with it for ever.'[1]

'Virtue', says Meyer Fortes about the Tallensi, 'is a question of moral relationships not of good deeds'. The good man is peaceable and honest, dignified and frank, kindly and generous. All these qualities are summed up by the Baganda in the untranslatable term *obuntu obulamu* – the living essence of humanity, what Man is meant to be. This and its opposite, that sinfulness which the true conscience of Africa condemns, is clearly portrayed in a remarkable document, The Laws of the Lumpa Church, which the 'prophet' Alice Lenshina promulgated for her followers in Northern Rhodesia. The first two laws condemn unruly lawlessness and racial discrimination. Then follows:

(3) Every Christian must not be in the following habits: (*a*) Backbiting, (*b*) insult, (*c*) lies, (*d*) pride, (*e*) boasting, (*f*) hatred, (*g*) anger, (*h*) harsh, (*i*) false witness, (*j*) selfish, (*k*) rudeness, (*l*) cunning, (*m*) stealing, and etc. He must be sincere, kind, trustworthy, love, patient and truthful.

(4) Every Christian must keep away from the following: coveting, witchcraft, stealing, adultery, sorcery, witches, drunkenness, bad songs and all primitive dances.

(5) Every Christian must have good manners of the public and in private. . . .[2]

[1] J. Middleton, *Lugbara Religion*, pp. 22–3.
[2] Transcribed by Dr Dorothea Lehmann in *Christians of the Copperbelt*, p. 253.

That ethics are essentially social is revealed also in the comments which loyal church elders make in an unguarded moment. 'If you drink and then go home and sleep it off, there is no trouble at all, but if you become quarrelsome, then you are bad.' Kasitile, the priest, convicted by the Christians, is blamed not for polygamy as such but because he loves one wife and squabbles with the rest. One of the points of deepest misunderstanding has been the European's constant failure to recognize that in Africa the sinfulness of so-called sexual sins does not reside in their sexuality, but in the fact that the dangerous intensity of the act is channelled against the proper structure of the family and becomes an attack against its members. So the adultery of a husband is thought to endanger the life of his wife or his unborn child; and, if a miner is killed underground, his wife is often cruelly punished for the unfaithfulness that is supposed to have made him vulnerable.

It is important, also, to understand that the degree of goodness or sinfulness in an action is not estimated in terms of the material act itself but in terms of its psychic effects upon another person. Father Placide Tempels tells the story of a village headman to whom a man from the neighbouring village of Busangu entrusted a young sheep. When the headman's dog was found eating the remains of the sheep, he gave the other man as compensation, first one sheep, then a second and a third, and finally a hundred francs also. Jahn explains, 'He gave what according to the European view was such enormous compensation because the man from Busangu said: "The

The Destroyer

loss of my sheep pains me, it gives me sorrow". After the reparation by one sheep he was still suffering. Only after he had had three sheep and a hundred francs could he forget his sorrow, and feel himself once more a living, happy man, only then was his life-force, his *magara*, restored.'[1]

This, then, is the meaning of the definition of sin as 'destruction'. It is the attitude of heart and mind which destroys or spoils the life-force of another, and especially the life-force of the family group. The Luganda translation of the central phrase in the Lord's Prayer, means literally – 'Forgive us our despoiling as we forgive them that despoil us.' This concept is implicit in all the fundamental metaphors in which, traditionally, Africa has expressed her understanding of sin. Theology is so largely a matter of metaphors that when a few of them recur in many different parts of a continent we should seize upon them as a kind of Rosetta Stone of spiritual communication.

For example, among all the southern Bantu, the idea of 'Shadow' (*sehihi, muridi*), is used of the evil influence of a person or an event which attacks the life-force of another in such a way as to diminish the moral rather than the physical powers. One upon whom Shadow falls is a person 'whose whole nature is changed . . . there is an overshadowing of the true relationships of life, and a deterioration of character, as when a child neglects or repudiates his duty to his parents, or a parent fails in his duty as such, or when a subject treats as of little concern

[1] P. Tempels, *Bantoe-Filosofie*, Antwerp 1946, pp. 89ff.

183

his allegiance to his chief'.[1] The evil force may often seem to be reduced to merely ritual impurity. Someone's death brings Shadow over the homestead, its inhabitants and belongings; a boy attending the initiation school without the proper ritual preparation will overshadow the other novices, making them dull and stupid. But this should not hide the true significance of the metaphor which 'is not a real or mystical shadow in our sense of the term, but an evil and contagious force conceptualized, on the analogy of a shadow, as an invisible counterpart of certain conditions'.[2]

The same idea is also conveyed in the metaphor of Weight. This also can appear to signify no more than ritual taboo, as when a pregnant woman is forbidden to touch 'medicines' lest she 'trample down' their power. But even that contains the idea of destroying the life-force. Weight, more than Shadow, depicts a deliberate and personal attack and is particularly associated with the brooding anger of witchcraft. When the Lugbara father broods over the rebellion of his son, the shades 'see his heart is *heavy*'. Kasitile, the priest of the Nyakyusa, spoke often of 'the heavy ones, the witches'; and the chiefs of that tribe are invested with a medicine to make them 'heavy with a power perilously like that of witchcraft'. After a death the children of the deceased are ritually protected to prevent them being trampled down by the angry shade. It is probably this concept which underlies

[1] J. T. Brown, *Among the Bantu Nomads*, Seeley Service 1926, pp. 137–8.
[2] J. D. and E. J. Krige in *African Worlds*, p. 70.

184

The Destroyer

the odd rule of the Temne of Sierra Leone that if anyone sits on the rice-mortar on a farm he must carry it a certain distance on his head, in order to undo any evil influence which he may have intended by putting his weight upon it.

The most widely used metaphor of evil is that of Heat. It is a complex derived from the two ideas of anger and drought. The Kriges have explained this concept among the Lovedu.

To them the ultimate good is rain. Rain is regarded as not merely the material source of life and happiness and the physical basis of man's sense of security; it is also a symbol of spiritual well-being and a manifestation that the social order is operating smoothly. Hence coolness denotes a state of euphoria: man and matter to be in order and to function properly have to be kept cool; angry ancestors must be cooled by means of medicine; even witches can be cooled and so made to forget their evil purposes. On the other hand heat as the antithesis of the main basis of man's security, the cooling, life-giving rain, is conceived as a destructive force leading to a state of dysphoria.[1]

Once again we meet many applications of the metaphor to what appears to be merely a taboo. Menstruation, sexual intercourse, childbirth, abortion, twin births, bereavement, are all thought to produce a condition of 'heat' and to call for a ritual cooling. But the underlying idea is always of impulse or emotion that is destructive because it is uncontrollable and smouldering. Among the Lugbara it is said:

[1] Idem, p. 68.

185

When a man goes to *awi* (sacrifice) he must remain peaceful, without a hot heart. He must stay thus for at least a day. If he quarrels on that day or is hot in his heart he becomes sick and *destroys the words* of the lineage and of the sacrifice.[1]

The Luhya think that the recently dead are 'hot', not yet reconciled to their changed status, while many tribes speak of recovery from sickness as 'being cooled'. Dr Pauw tells of a Christian woman, wife of an evangelist, who, when saying grace, prayed God to give the food 'with cool hands'. He also reports an account of the rain ritual among the Tswana, showing how the metaphor is expressed in symbolic form. A black beast was slaughtered as a gift for the ancestors. 'Young immature girls had to bring water and driftwood from the river. The driftwood and the contents of the slaughtered animal's stomach were burnt. The water, over which a prayer had been said for the help of God and the "fathers", . . . was sprinkled on the fire to produce clouds of smoke.' Water and driftwood from the river are associated with coolness, as also the green vegetable matter from the stomach, the young girls have the coolness of innocence, and the smoke clouds symbolize the rain clouds, 'clouds of coolness', which were desired.[2]

The power of innocence is recognized in many African rituals. When the *Mugwe* of the Tigania Meru prays for rain he offers sacrifice beside a pool in the heart of the forest. If the first time fails he goes again accompanied by a small, innocent girl dressed in a skin cloth. Purity is

[1] J. Middleton, op. cit., p. 119.
[2] B. A. Pauw, *Religion in a Tswana Chiefdom*, pp. 35, 149.

The Destroyer

also, as we have seen, an essential quality of the *Mugwe* himself. This is, in fact, the fourth of the great metaphors of goodness and sin. But it would be misleading to read into it the same nuances that the word 'purity' carries either in the Bible or in English usage. At bottom it bears the same connotation as the other three concepts, and the four metaphors are interchangeable – overshadowing, weighing down, heat and dirt – all depicting that antagonism to the life-force in others which is the essence of sin in the primal view. After a burial the Baganda use the cool juice of a young banana stem, the southern Bantu that of a succulent bulb, to wash off the contamination or the *khitshila*, 'dirt', of death which, as we have seen, is the potential envy of the recently deceased. Once a year the men and boys of the Temne villages visit the shrine hut in which lie the stones that represent the ancestral heads of every family. These are washed and covered with a white cloth – symbolically cooling and purifying any anger they may be cherishing against the living. In the ceremony of cleansing the hearth the Nyakyusa say that 'to clear out the ashes means they take away all that dirt, the dirt which the witches have brought and the shades; it is the cause of illness'.[1] The Lugbara explain that 'the work of an elder is to keep the territory without trouble so that the home may be *clean*, so that death, sickness and evil words do not enter into the homesteads and people live peaceably and quietly'.[2]

This, then, is the area in which a genuine sense of sin is to be looked for in Africa. This is the felt need to which

[1] Monica Wilson, op. cit., p. 103.   [2] J. Middleton, op. cit., p. 39.

187

the gospel of salvation must speak if it is to be an authentic Good News. Monica Wilson writes:

In analysing the rituals of the Nyakyusa, I have been driven to the conclusion that they are in fact dogged by a sense of guilt, for this is the only hypothesis on which the linking of misfortune and sin, the preoccupation with 'filth', and the recurring acts of purification can be explained. One of the sources of this sense of guilt is, I suggest, awareness of anger within, for it is believed that such anger injures others. An act of confession is essential to many rituals, and what must be confessed are anger, hard thoughts, ill-will against others. The anger is acknowledged to come primarily from men – it is the angry parent who rouses the shades to action by muttering over the fire – but the guilt, the filth, is projected on to the shade or the hero. It is when they 'brood on' men that men are contaminated. A shade or a man that is *ngolofu* – good, righteous – is one without a grudge, without anger against anyone, free of witchcraft, and free of sex transgression – 'there is no accusation against him'.[1]

The primal vision is quite clear about the Kingdom of God: it is a community of the living and the dead that is purified of all destructive antagonisms. It is for this that the Dinka sing their plea to the hero-gods.

ABUK, mother of DENG
Leave your home in the sky and come to work in our homes,
Make our country become clean like the original home of
   DENG,
Come make our country as one: the country of Akwol
Is not as one, either by night or by day.
The child called Deng, his face has become sad,
The children of Akwol have bewildered their chief's mind.[2]

[1] Monica Wilson, op. cit., p. 161.
[2] Godfrey Lienhardt, *Divinity and Experience*, p. 103.

The Destroyer

It is in the area of the closest human relationships, those between father and son, between husband and wife and their respective relations, and between the several wives of a polygamist, that the greatest danger of antagonism lies and the deepest sense of guilt. We have already seen how long an adult son is compelled to remain dependent on his father and submissive to his authority, and how the father-son conflict contributes to the status of deceased parents and grandparents through the sense of guilt which has accumulated in the successor generation. Lienhardt goes so far as to suggest that this is projected into man's understanding of his relationship to God. Their separation is felt to correspond to the separation of the adult son from his father's household, and produces the same submerged guilt. An old Dinka singer explained the sacrifices in this way, saying, 'It is what a man does when he has quarrelled with his father or his elder brother, he will give him something to wash away the anger from his heart.'[1]

The most intense hatreds can be generated also between women married to the same husband, and it is strange that Africa has devised so few precautionary avoidance-rules in this relationship. One can sympathize with the seething jealousy of a favourite but childless wife who, as she prepares her husband's food, has to listen to a junior co-wife crooning over her latest baby:

Someone would like to have you for her child
But you are my own.
Someone wished she had you to nurse you on a good mat;

[1] Idem, p. 44.

189

Someone wished you were hers; she would put you on a camel blanket;
But I have you to rear you on a torn mat.
Someone wished she had you, but I have you.[1]

It is not surprising therefore that many of the allegations, or self-accusations, of witchcraft and cursing occur within these close relationships. For example, the Lugbara say:

A man loves his child, he must teach him good actions. Perhaps he must strike him, perhaps he must ask the ghosts to strike for him, if that child is big. . . . A youth will not have shame, but a man who has a wife and children . . . will get shame. . . . Perhaps he thinks in his heart that his father is bad. Then he may refuse his father, and think that his father has forgotten the words of blood (kinship) and think his father to be a witch.[2]

Witchcraft is the active embodiment of that brooding anger which in Africa is the essence of sin. The universal dread of it comes from the knowledge that when anger of that kind goes forth from the heart it quickly passes the point of recall. It is at large in the world with an autonomy and power of its own. A man fears his own anger almost as deeply as the anger of others, and either fear can eat away at his vitality and destroy his life-force. A Christian woman, the wife of a chief, once asked Monica Wilson,

About that choking of which I was telling you, what do *you* think it is when you wake up with pains like that? I'll tell you

[1] Akan cradle song quoted by K. Nketia, *Black Orpheus*, No. 3 1958, Ibadan.　　[2] Quoted by J. Middleton, op. cit., p. 227.

The Destroyer

how it was. I went to see my sister, and found her very ill. She had had a miscarriage and her in-laws had not looked after her properly, they had not sent her to hospital, and when she was lying ill her mother-in-law even refused to come and cook for her. And so I was very very angry with them. And that night I woke up feeling as if someone were stamping on my head, and I heard the knocking on the door and the footsteps I told you about. What do you make of such things when you dream someone strikes you or is throttling you?[1]

Dr Field and Dr Debrunner both report from Ghana numbers of pathetic cases of self-accused witches, mostly women whose frustration and resentment has turned to reactive depression. A woman in a polygamous household believes she has made her co-wife barren. The sister of a handsome carpenter confesses that she has rendered him impotent because he once refused to make a door for her. A middle-aged woman, whose unhappy marriage had ended in divorce, and five of whose seven children had died, the two survivors living with their father, taxes herself with every death in the family for the past twenty years.

The inward loneliness of so many of these cases is typical of the state of mind which is everywhere associated with a witch. This is not the simple anger which explodes in an outburst or a blow, but a solitary and sullen indignation, which the Lugbara call *ole*.

The typical situation in which a man feels *ole* is said to be when he passes a homestead and sees the occupants sitting eating, with good millet in its flat basket and with pots of rich and succulent meats and relishes, and he is not called in to

[1] Monica Wilson, op. cit., p. 183.

191

share the meal. A man also feels *ole* when he sees another showing off his agility at a dance, being admired by girls and other young men while he stands alone. A man feels *ole* when he sees the wealth of another's home, the fertility of his wives and livestock, while he is poor and his own children and livestock few and ailing. Or a man who wishes to seduce the wives and daughters of other men, may feel *ole* against their guardians who prevent his doing so. Then in his heart he hates the other whom he thinks of as in some way harming him. . . . A man who sits alone and above all eats alone is always thought to be a witch. Therefore witches often pretend to be chatty and friendly and generous to everyone.[1]

This is the ultimate horror and darkness of the primal world-view, that beneath the smiling face may lurk the hating heart. The traditional African community, for all its solidarity and the truth of its vision of Man, is corrupted by a twofold mistrust – mistrust of the stranger because he is outside the kinship bond, and mistrust of the unknown witch because he is outside humanity. He has become the Un-man, the Outsider, whose very existence testifies to an area beyond the ancestral scope where neither the criteria of the created world nor the authority of God himself have any bearing. This is the hell of isolation that we have already glimpsed outside the solidarity of Man, and angry antagonism is the force that drives a person out beyond the point of no return. 'The motives of the witch', says Margaret Field, 'are felt to belong to a monstrous, sinister order of things that transcends comprehensible goodness and badness.'[2] In

[1] J. Middleton, op. cit., pp. 240, 242.
[2] M. J. Field, *Religion and Medicine of the Ga people*, p. 160.

192

The Destroyer

the words of a Temne Christian of Sierra Leone, who
might be speaking for every tribe in Africa,

All my people believe in witchcraft. The world of witches is a
different plane of existence from the human one, but there
are those living in the world who have recourse to that world
by night, and they are able to do very terrible things. Truly
witchcraft is the basic fear of all my people; and you will
never understand the Temne people unless you believe this.[1]

If the servant of the Gospel has entered so far into the
primal world-view that he no longer confuses its light
with its darkness, he will see clearly how his Master is
the Light of the whole world's light and the Liberator
from its every darkness. Christ is supremely relevant to
African need, if only that need, and not some imagined
one, is brought to him.

The Good News consists first in the fact that the
dominion of this gentle Lord is total. There are no
strangers and no realms of terror that lie beyond his
sovereignty. His all-world power, having all the clans of
mankind in its keeping, can be trusted against every
imaginable antagonism. To the 'Outsider' himself he
brings an understanding that banishes loneliness and a
reconciliation patient enough to subdue the ultimate
enmity. His method here will be largely Africa's own —
the way of confession, absolution, exorcism and reparation. It is a serious condemnation of many 'mission'
hospitals that numbers of patients who, failing to settle
down, discharge themselves after a few days, are to be
found the next day at some shrine confessing the sins

[1] From a manuscript in the author's possession.

about which the Christian doctor never thought to enquire. 'When a sick child is brought to a shrine', says Dr Field, 'the priest invariably seeks first for strife between the parents.' She also points out that 'some tribes begin their annual festivals with a day of peacemaking on which people seek out their friends and relatives and confess not only their misdeeds but also any secret resentments they have harboured'.[1] In southern Tanganyika also 'men become *mwelu*, pure, by confession; "speaking out" is a condition of efficacy in sacrifice and the officiant blows out water as a symbol of bringing up all the anger that was in his heart'.[2] Confession followed by sacrifice and exorcism is an invariable part in the treatment of any self-accused witch. It is significant, too, that so many of the independent Churches, and also revival movements within the 'orthodox' Churches, make great use of confession in one way or another. The African concept of group solidarity may demand some form of 'open' confession within the fellowship, as well as private confession in the presence of a priest, in order to satisfy the troubled conscience and reinstate the penitent.

The Gospel, however, is more than a protective charm, more than a pastoral technique. It meets the ultimate point of need in the African world-view by bringing together two factors which African thought has never considered in the same frame of reference, namely God and the destructive antagonism of sin. Here and there a few steps have been taken towards that intolerable

---

[1] M. J. Field, *Search for Security*, pp. 113, 118, 119.
[2] Monica Wilson, op. cit., p. 163.

The Destroyer

juxtaposition, but they all stopped far short, as every other philosophy in Man's long search has done. Yet the truth, which Christians themselves can hardly believe, answers so perfectly to the unanswerable flaw in the primal view. Because God is the All-Present who exists eternally for others, every sin which attacks the life-force of another despoils him. He is the Author of the moral law because he is the Victim of every breach of it. Every conflict is against him; all the brooding anger from the heart of Man, let loose in the world as an independent force of destruction, falls upon him. At the heart of the totality stands the Cross, cosmic because it is the Creator who hangs upon it. There the love of God bears the sin of the world and every curse dies out on him. God forgives the transgression and antagonism of our race, submitting to the evil of it until it is swallowed up and submerged in fathomless love. The shadow menaces him and is dispelled by his perfection; the weight tramples him down and is carried by his strength; the heat of enmity is assuaged in the coolness of his peace, and its filthy contagion cleansed by his blood. In the midst of the world man's eternal Neighbour has died for him and risen again.

13

The Practice of the Presence

Da suya da daffua da kyapa duk labarin wuta su ke ji, gasshi shi ya ga wuta kirikiri (Hausa)
Frying, boiling and parching hear news of fire, but roasting sees fire face to face

>>>◆<<<

THIS, like other books in the same series, is an attempt to explore an approach to men of another faith and culture which is reverent and attentive, and which consists essentially not of assertion, nor even of action, but of presence. If the preceding chapters have had any validity they point to the peculiar rightness of such an approach in Africa. The core of Africa's wisdom is that she knows the difference between existence and presence. 'Europeans', they say, 'are people who do not greet one another in the street.' It is easy to excuse ourselves by pointing at the congestion in Oxford Street, but that is only to endorse their critique of such a civilization. For we ourselves know what it means, as a stranger passes us on the pavement, to catch a fleeting, spontaneous smile and to know we are recognized not by name but simply for our humanity. For a moment our presence to one another, eye to eye and face to face, dispels the isolation and lifts our hearts.

Africans believe that presence is the debt they owe to

196

The Practice of the Presence

one another. That is why Nantume the schoolgirl came to sit silently as I ironed my clothes that day, and ended her visit as all such visits are closed, with the words, 'I have seen you.' Not to be seen, not to be recognized, to become invisible and anonymous, is the burden that subverts the integrity of all those whom the city swallows.

The primal vision is of a world of presences, of face-to-face meeting not only with the living but just as vividly with the dead and with the whole totality of nature. It is a universe of I and Thou. Let us not sentimentalize. Africa does not achieve this sensitive receptivity toward the other person all the time. There are many dull and blind and callous, and the range of their awareness is limited, as we have seen. But the vision is there and the longing is everywhere alive – which is more than we of the West can say.

The Christian, whoever he may be, who stands in that world in the name of Christ, has nothing to offer unless he offers to be present, really and totally present, really and totally *in* the present. The failure of so many 'professional' Christians has been that they are 'not all there'!

In the first place this means simply friendship, unassuming and undemanding, offered to the other man. 'We come into his presence, not he into ours. He will feel the same way. If we strain to show off before him, we shall miss him. If we try to control him, he will fade away. No matter how familiar and good to us, presence is elusive. Its spontaneity rebuffs all forced intimacy.'[1] If one offers such friendship in Africa, in spite of all the

[1] Ralph Harper, *The Sleeping Beauty*, Harvill 1956, p. 122.

rising barriers of disillusionment and mistrust, it is likely to be met with the same response that Saint-Exupéry expressed in his *Letter to a Hostage,* which is so extraordinarily relevant to relationships in Africa at the present time.

My friend, I need your friendship. I am weary of all these controversies, of all these refusals to listen to the other man, of all the fanaticisms! I can go to you without dressing up in a uniform, or having to listen to the recitation of any Koran, or having to give up any part of what is inside me. When I am with you there is no need for me to be for ever defending my ideas or my conduct, no need to plead my case, no need to prove I am right; I find peace. . . . Over and beyond my clumsy expressions and the arguments with which I may be deceiving myself, you merely consider the man in me. You respect me as the exponent of certain beliefs, customs, loves and loyalties, and my difference from you, far from diminishing you, gives you increase. Your questions are those one puts to a traveller.[1]

A humble reverence that never desires to manipulate or possess or use the other is always a feature of the face-to-face encounter of true presence, and therefore it flourishes in silence. Ralph Harper, whose exquisite book, *The Sleeping Beauty,* has done so much to illumine the world of presence, has this to say:

Each order of experience has its own atmosphere. The atmosphere of presence, of giving, of wholeness, is silence. We know that serious things have to be done in silence, because we do not have words to measure the immeasurable. In

[1] Quoted in *Iesus Caritas,* Association Charles de Jésus, Paris 1958, p. 97.

The Practice of the Presence

silence men love, pray, listen, compose, paint, write, think, suffer. These experiences are all occasions of giving and receiving, of some encounter with forces that are inexhaustible and independent of us. These are easily distinguishable from our routines and possessiveness as silence is distinct from noise.[1]

In contrast to the silence of God how much of the mission of his Church seems to be contrived in 'routines and possessiveness'! As Harper goes on to say, 'All men choose either compassion or jabbering. The more we chatter, the busier we seem, but the farther from God's silence and God's Word.' Those who have lost the capacity for listening, who cannot be there for others, are unable even to be truly present to themselves. In their busy self-assertion they never meet themselves; they are distracted, strained, dispersed. Only the silence, only the practice of the presence of God, in sacrament and meditation, in a steady painful flowering of sensitivity to all presences, can restore and integrate so that given-ness can be maintained.

'Compassion' is the final operative word to define what the way of presence really means. It sums up the listening, responsive, agonizing receptivity of the prophet and the poet. For it is impossible to be open and sensitive in one direction without being open to all. If a man would open his heart towards his fellow he must keep it open to all other comers – to the stranger, to the dead, to the enchanting and awful presences of nature, to powers of beauty and terror, to the pain and anxiety of men, to the

[1] Ralph Harper, op. cit., p. 111.

199

menace and catastrophe of our time, and to the over-whelming presence of God. So many of our Eucharists fall short of the glory of God because, while purporting to concentrate on the Real Presence of Christ, they seem to be oblivious to the real presence of men, either in the worshipping family or in the world around. To present oneself to God means to expose oneself, in an intense and vulnerable awareness, not only to him but to all that is. And this is what, apart from Christ, we dare not do. Presence is too much for us to face.

In Dahomey a married man with children of his own is forbidden to use the same gateway to the homestead as his father, lest they meet face to face, life-force against life-force. By the same precaution, to avoid a direct encounter, Man has tried to relegate God to a separate realm of existence. This is the truth that seems to emerge undeniably from a study of the primal vision. The celestial God whose divinity consists in kingly authority raised to an Olympian degree of remoteness is a man-made God, and in Africa we have actually seen the process taking place. And the more remote God is made to appear the greater is the need for magic. If his hand is not there to protect and heal, if his eyes are indifferent to the mustering of the forces of darkness, then charms and spells and curses must be enlisted against them. Some see in the story of the coming of the magi to Bethlehem the representative magicians of that ancient world surrendering the instruments of their craft to the incarnate God. Only Immanuel – God himself involved in every contingency – can render magic unnecessary.

The Practice of the Presence

The God whom, all along, Africa has guessed at and dreamed of, is One who is always and wholly present for every part of his creation. His transcendence has been too spatially conceived. It must be looked for in the quality of his love, and love, as Brunner has said, is 'being there for others'. In his sovereign will he created the universe by committing himself to it. The absolute difference between himself and all other is that his very nature is to give himself totally while remaining inexhaustibly himself. The bush burning but not consumed, the widow's cruse of oil, the loaves and fishes, the Eucharistic Bread and Wine – these are the true symbols of his relationship to the created world.

In Africa, as elsewhere, speculation about the existence of God may be less true than the sense of the presence of God, that Presence which mysteriously takes the initiative and, under many forms, suddenly confronts Man on the road. 'For,' says Irenaeus, 'as they who see the light are within the light and perceive its brilliancy, so they who see God are within God as they behold his splendour.'[1]

Something of this is implicit, as we have seen, in the Bushman's story of *Dxui*. It is echoed, also, in the astonishing answer given by a Tswana to David Livingstone's question, What is holiness (*boitsepho*)?

When copious showers have descended during the night, and all the earth and leaves and cattle are washed clean and the sun rising shows a drop of dew on every blade of grass, and the air breathes fresh, that is holiness.[2]

Many of the fathers of Eastern and Celtic monasticism

[1] Irenaeus, *Adv. Haer.*, iv.20.7.
[2] D. Livingstone, *Expedition to the Zambesi*, Murray, 1865, p. 64.

201

might have said the same. So also would at least one of
the great Jewish rabbinic schools.

A heathen asked Rabbi Joshua ben Karka, Why did God
speak to Moses from the thorn bush? Rabbi Joshua replied, If
he had spoken from a carob tree or from a sycamore you
would have asked me the same question! But so as not to
dismiss you without an answer, God spoke from the thorn
bush to teach you that there is no place where the Shekinah
is not, not even a thorn bush.[1]

Yet he might have said that a bush of thorns is the
very place where one should most expect to see the full
glory of the given-ness of God. For the Cross is the measure of his self-commitment to the creation. It is the price
of his patient, unpossessive friendship towards Mankind.
Its three hours of silence summed up all the long aeons of
his watch for Man's return; its loneliness was the deso-
lation of a presence endlessly rebuffed, unrecognized,
anonymous; its agony contained his eternal compassion
toward the bent world. Middleton Murry, in his com-
mentary on the letters of Keats, speaks of this attitude
of enduring presence toward the mystery and paradox
of existence.

'For this other kind of forgiveness,' he says 'a forgiveness which forgives not only man, but life itself, not only
the pains which men inflict but the pains which are knit
up with the very nature of existence, we have no word.
Let it be called . . . Acceptance.'[2] One would add that the

---

[1] C. G. Montefiore and H. Loewe, *A Rabbinic Anthology*, Mac-
millan 1938, p. 13.

[2] Quoted by 'Nicodemus', *Renascence*, Faber 1943, p. 60.

The Practice of the Presence

Cross affirms that the divine acceptance is not complacency; it is acceptance of final involvement and responsibility.

Yet, intense as is his divine receptivity toward every sin and every pain in every creature, he is present also with vivid awareness towards all beauty, all faith, all achievement. For the joy that is set before him he endures, and his presence is vibrant with triumph and resurrection.

That is the tremendous Presence in the midst of the world from which our first parents hid themselves and from which Cain went forth into loneliness. That is the Presence which Moses knew, eye to eye and face to face, without which the building of the Chosen Community had no significance or attraction. That is the Presence which is promised unto the end of the world to those who go to disciple all the nations. And this alone is their warrant for believing that the way of presence is not merely a new missionary method, but God's own way of drawing Adam into his embrace and lifting the despoiled and threatened Creation up into his peace.

There have been a few moments in the history of the Church since the writing of the epistles to the Ephesians and the Colossians when men have built their faith upon this understanding of God. Irenaeus was one such, and the great Celtic saints followed in the same path. The eighth-century writer of the famous 'Deer's Cry', which we know as St Patrick's Breastplate, invoked in one prayer all the presences that met him with grace in the world of sense and of spirit. It sums up and contains all

the spiritual awareness of the primal vision and lifts it
into the fulness of Christ. Would that it were translated
and sung in every tongue of Africa!

I arise today
Through a mighty strength, the invocation of the Trinity
Through belief in the threeness
Through confession of the oneness
Of the Creator of Creation.

I arise today
Through the strength of Christ's birth with His baptism,
Through the strength of His crucifixion with His burial,
Through the strength of His resurrection with His ascension,
Through the strength of His coming down for Judgement.

I arise today
Through the strength of the love of Cherubim,
In obedience of angels,
In the service of archangels,
In prayers of ancestors,
In predictions of prophets,
In preachings of apostles,
In faith of confessors,
In deeds of righteous men. .

I arise today
Through the strength of heaven; –
Light of sun,
Radiance of moon,
Splendour of fire,
Speed of lightening,
Swiftness of wind,
Depth of sea,
Stability of earth,
Firmness of rock.

204

The Practice of the Presence

I arise today
Through God's strength to pilot me,
God's might to uphold me,
God's wisdom to guide me,
God's hand to guard me,
God's shield to protect me,
God's host to save me,
From snares of devils,
From temptations of vices,
From all who shall wish me ill,
Afar and near,
Alone and in multitude.

I summon today all these powers between me and those evils,
Against every cruel merciless power that may oppose my
*   body and soul,*
Against incantations of false prophets,
Against black laws of pagandom,
Against spells of witches,
Against every knowledge that corrupts man's body and soul.

Christ to shield me this day
So that there come to me abundance of reward.
Christ with me, Christ before me, Christ behind me,
Christ in me, Christ beneath me, Christ above me,
Christ when I lie down, Christ when I sit, Christ when I
*   arise,*
Christ in the heart of every man who thinks of me,
Christ in the mouth of everyone who speaks of me,
Christ in every eye that sees me,
Christ in every ear that hears me.[1]

[1] Translation by Kuno Meyer, *Selections from Ancient Irish Poetry* (2nd ed.), Constable 1913, p. 25.

Short Bibliography

Achebe, Chinua, *Things fall apart*, Heinemann, 1958.

Beier, H. Ulli (editor of), *Black Orpheus*, Ibadan.

Beier, H. Ulli, *The Egungun Cult* in 'Nigeria', No. 51, Lagos, 1956.

Bernadi, B., *The Mugwe*, Oxford, 1959.

Beti, Mongo, *Le Pauvre Christ de Bomba*.

Callaway, H., *The Religious System of the Amazulu*, Natal, 1868-70.

Carothers, J. C., *The African Mind in Health and Disease*, World Health Organization, Geneva, 1953.

Danquah, J. B., *The Akan Doctrine of God*, Lutterworth, 1944.

Debrunner, H., *Witchcraft in Ghana*, Kumasi, 1959.

Dieterlen, Germaine, *Essai sur la religion bambara*, Paris, 1950.

Dodds, E. R., *The Greeks and the Irrational*, Univ. of California Press, 1951.

Ekwensi, Cyprian, *People of the City*, Andrew Dakers, 1954.

Evans-Pritchard, E. E., *Witchcraft, Oracles and Magic among the Azande*, Oxford, 1937.

Evans-Pritchard, E. E., *The Nuer*, Oxford, 1940.

Field, M. J., *Religion and Medicine of the Ga People*, Oxford, 1937.

Field, M. J., *Search for Security*, Faber, 1960.

Forde, Daryll (editor of), *African Worlds*, Oxford, 1954.

Fortes, Meyer, *Oedipus and Job in West African Religion*, Oxford, 1959.

Gbadamosi, B. and Beier, Ulli, *Yoruba Poetry*, Ibadan, 1959.

206

Short Bibliography

Gelfand, Michael, *Medicine and Magic of the Mashona*, Juta, Johannesburg, 1956.

Gelfand, Michael, *Shona Ritual*, Juta, Johannesburg, 1959.

Griaule, Marcel, *Dieu d'eau*, Paris, 1948.

Hadfield, P., *Traits of Divine Kingship in Africa*, Watts, 1949.

Idowu, E. B., *Olodumare, God in Yoruba Belief*, Longmans, 1962.

Jahn, Janheinz, *Muntu*, Faber, 1961.

Kegame, Alexis, *La Philosophie Bantu-Rwondaise de l'Etre*, Brussels, 1956.

Kenyatta, J., *Facing Mount Kenya*, Secker and Warburg, 1938.

Kidd, D., *Savage Childhood*, Black, 1906.

Lehmann, D. and Taylor, J. V., *Christians of the Copperbelt*, SCM Press, 1961.

Lienhardt, Godfrey, *Divinity and Experience (The Religion of the Dinka)*, Oxford, 1961.

Lucas, Olumede, *The Religion of the Yoruba*, Lagos, 1948.

Mayer, P., *Witches* – Rhodes University paper, Grahamstown, 1951.

Middleton, J., *Lugbara Religion*, Oxford, 1960.

Meyerowitz, E., *The Sacred State of the Akan*, Faber, 1951.

Le Monde Noir (special issue of nos. 8-9 of *Présence Africaine*), Paris, 1950.

Mopeli-Paulus, A. S. and Basner, M., *Turn to the Dark*, Cape, 1956.

Mphahlele, Ezekiel, *Down Second Avenue*, Faber, 1959.

Nadel, S. F., *Nupe Religion*, Routledge, 1954.

Parrinder, Godfrey, *West African Religion*, Oxford, 1949.

Parrinder, Godfrey, *Religion in an African City*, Oxford, 1953.

Parrinder, Godfrey, *African Traditional Religion*, Hutchinson, 1954.

Pauw, B. A., *Religion in a Tswana Chiefdom*, Oxford, 1960.

Post, Laurens van der, *The Lost Land of the Kalahari*, Hogarth, 1959.

Post, Laurens van der, *The Heart of the Hunter*, Hogarth, 1961.

Présence Africaine – for two-volume account of the second Congress of African writers and artists, see *Le Monde Noir*.

Des Prêtres Noirs s'interrogent, Editions du Cerf, Paris, 1956.

Raum, O. T., *Chaga Childhood*, Oxford, 1940.

Richards, A. I., *Hunger and Work in a Savage Tribe*, Routledge, 1932.

Richards, A. I., *East African Chiefs*, Faber, 1960.

Schapera, I., *The Tswana*, International African Institute, 1954.

Seligman, C. G. and B. Z., *Pagan Tribes of the Nilotic Sudan*, Routledge, 1932.

Senghor, L. S., *Chants d'ombre*, Paris, 1954.

Senghor, L. S., *Anthologie de la poésie nègre et malgache*, Paris, 1948.

Smith, Edwin W. (editor of), *African Ideas of God*, Edinburgh House Press, 1959.

Sundkler, Bengt, *The Christian Ministry in Africa*, Upsala and SCM Press, 1960.

Taylor, J. V., *The Growth of the Church in Buganda*, SCM Press, 1958.

Tempels, Fr Placide, *La Philosophie Bantoue*, Editions Lovania, Elizabethville, 1945.

Tutuola, Amos, *My Life in the Bush of Ghosts*, Faber, 1954.

Tutuola, Amos, *Simbi and the Satyr of the Dark Jungle*, Faber, 1955.

Tutuola, Amos, *The Brave African Huntress*, Faber, 1958.

Welbourn, F. B., *East African Rebels*, SCM Press, 1961.

Westermann, D., *Africa and Christianity*, Oxford, 1937.

Wilson, Monica, *Rituals of Kingship among the Nyakyusa*, Oxford, 1956.

Wilson, Monica, *Communal Rituals of the Nyakyusa*, Oxford, 1959.

Young, T. Cullen, *African Ways and Wisdom*, Lutterworth, 1937.

Index

Abraham, 119, 122, 123

Adam, 122-6, 171

African religion, survival of, 27-9

Africanization of worship, 21-5

Akan (major ethnic group, Ghana, Ivory Coast, and Mali), 27, 62, 77, 81, 98, 100, 143, 178

Ambo (tribe, S.W. Africa), 83, 87

Ancestors, 98, 100-101, 112, 121, 132, 136, 146-7, 151, 158, 162, 167, 171, 180, 204

Anger, 48-9, 138, 181, 185-95

Ashanti (tribal division of Akan, *q.v.*), 49, 87, 136

Bemba (tribe, N. Rhodesia), 54, 163

Bridewealth, 96, 110-11

Burundi, 84, 87

Bushmen (aboriginal ethnic group S. Africa), 72, 76, 91, 201

Chagga (tribe near Mt Kilimanjaro), 98, 100-102

Chiefs, 39, 80, 133, 135-44

Childlessness, 100, 111, 189

Children, 15, 20, 51-4, 95-8, 100-102

Christian worship, 20-23, 169-70, 194

Circumcision, 102, 114, 125

Cleansing, 126, 187-9, 195

Communion, Holy, 170, 200

Communion with the dead, 169-71

Confession, 41, 49, 188, 191, 193, 194

Conscience, 56, 58, 177-8, 194

Cross, The, 35, 92, 132, 195, 202-3

Curses, 180, 190, 195

Dahomey, 96, 140, 179, 200

Destiny, 47-8, 62-3, 100, 177-8

Dinka (tribe, S. Sudan), 45, 56-7, 59, 77, 82, 86, 96, 108, 136-7, 139, 143-4, 161, 170, 175, 189

Index

DATE DUE

AP 28 69			
GAYLORD			PRINTED IN U.S.A.

Printed in the USA
CPSIA information can be obtained
at www.ICGtesting.com
CBHW071946180824
13383CB00003B/27